Praise for *7 Rules of Power*

"In one word—incredible! Dr. Pfeffer has written the ultimate book on power that avoids the traps of conventional theories on leadership, and instead dives into the techniques that really change your life and career. Beautifully written and full of poignant stories and examples, *7 Rules of Power* is my recommended read for anyone looking to radically change the trajectory of their life for good."
—**Marshall Goldsmith, Thinkers 50 #1 Executive Coach and** *New York Times* **bestselling author of** *Mojo* **and** *What Got You Here Won't Get You There*

"Like a rousing slap of truth in the face, Pfeffer's tough-minded, capstone book on power identifies 7 research-based, reality-revealing rules for hierarchical success. Anyone hoping to rise within an organization needs to obtain power and, therefore, needs to read this brilliant book."
—**Robert Cialdini,** *New York Times* **bestselling author of** *Influence* **and** *Pre-Suasion*

"*7 Rules of Power* delivers easy-to-digest, practical tips for how you can be more powerful in your own life. Using real-life examples of individuals altering their lives by following his rules, Pfeffer delivers his message with humor and humanity. Pfeffer shows us how often we give away our power and how we can reclaim it. I was so inspired by Pfeffer's writing and his class that I wrote a book, *Take Back Your Power,* for women in workplaces not always set up for them. It is a tribute to all I have learned from Professor Pfeffer as both a mentor and coach over the past decade."
—**Deborah Liu, author of** *Take Back Your Power;* **CEO, Ancestry.com; board member, Intuit; former VP, Facebook; and founder, Women in Product**

"Jeff Pfeffer's latest leadership masterpiece is as brilliantly insightful as it is refreshingly candid and pragmatic, anchored in cutting edge scholarship. Pfeffer is the current Leonard Bernstein of leadership studies. There is simply no competitor to the highly readable, smart, wide-ranging take on power in *7 Rules of Power.*"
—**Jeffrey Sonnenfeld, founder and CEO of the Chief Executive Leadership Institute; Lester Crown Professor and Senior Associate Dean for Leadership Studies, Yale School of Management**

"Dr. Pfeffer's *7 Rules of Power* is a must read and highly useful for anyone at any stage of their career. The book offers a balanced, thoughtful view on what is an often uncomfortable topic for many people, especially women. Pfeffer is clear and to the point with practical, research-based steps for owning your power your way. It will stir your thinking and truly change your perspective."
—**Stacy Brown-Philpot, former CEO, TaskRabbit; Board Member, HP, Inc., and Nordstrom;** *Forbes* **40 under 40; former head of Google's online sales and operations in India**

"Jeff Pfeffer is the most honest teacher I've ever had. He is unafraid to say it like it is—a rare quality where people maintain pleasantries at the expense of the truth. The lessons from *7 Rules of Power* will take a lifetime to fully implement. The book provides the lens through which I view the decisions and behaviors of those around me. Most importantly, Pfeffer has taught me that to win the game, changing the rules trumps raw effort."

—Vivas Kumar, CEO and co-founder, Mitra Chem, Stanford GSB 2021

"When I started reading *7 Rules of Power,* I had a long list of assumptions about leadership and building influence. With each chapter, more pieces of the power puzzle fell into place. By trying the strategies from the book, I founded a consulting company where I leveraged my 20+ years of professional experience to provide research, innovation, and strategy advice. I am building my own brand as an effective executive coach. Through relentless networking, I have found powerful allies to break the rules and pursue a power-related Ph.D. My mantras are "Why not me? "Why not now?" Most importantly, "How can you tell whether something will work for you if you haven't tried it?"

—Monika Stezewska-Kruk, CEO, Corvus Innovation; Executive Coach and Facilitator; Stanford LEAD program graduate

"*7 Rules of Power* will shoot you to the moon and beyond. This book changed my life. A Nigerian woman, I work as a geoscientist in an Italian multinational energy company. Performance got me in, but power kept me ahead. I used principles from the book to build influence outside of my company. I built networks and became central. I received international awards and invitations to speak at top leadership forums. I was named among the most influential persons of African descent. I created a unique brand for myself, and now I represent my organization abroad. Usually the only black woman in the room, *7 Rules of Power* gave me an edge."

—Tosin Joel, Stanford LEAD; MIT Sloan Fellow; Director, Hack for Inclusion; founder, GTBOOL; Project Head, Eni

"Ideas from *7 Rules of Power* helped me design and live my dream career as a digital health expert. This book is a must-have for minorities and people seeking to have social impact, because we tend to shy away from the concept of power. *7 Rules* reframes power and provides tactical, practical tools to actually change the world!"

—Marta Milkowska, Stanford GSB 2020; Consultant at Boston Consulting Group; Interim CEO, Reveri Health; founder, Dtx Future; first Stanford platform on digital therapeutics

"The thing about power is that it will always exist. After a lifetime of being the collaborator, team player, and 'nice' person, Pfeffer's *7 Rules of Power* taught me that power is not about control or greed—it is about effectiveness. Gaining and using power allows us to effect the change we want in building a career, organization, or a world that aligns with our personal values. The lessons have been transformational in my venture capital career and continue to guide my personal and professional path."

—Laura Chau, Stanford GSB 2018; Partner, Canaan Partners; Forbes 30 Under 30, Board Member, Ollie Pets and Clutch

7
RULES OF POWER

Also by Jeffrey Pfeffer

Dying for a Paycheck

Leadership BS

Power: Why Some People Have It—and Others Don't

What Were They Thinking?
Unconventional Wisdom About Management

Hard Facts, Dangerous Half-Truths, and Total Nonsense:
Profiting from Evidence-Based Management (with Robert I. Sutton)

The Knowing-Doing Gap (with Robert I. Sutton)

Hidden Value: Achieving Extraordinary Results
with Ordinary People (with Charles A. O'Reilly)

The Human Equation: Building Profits by Putting People First

Competitive Advantage Through People

New Directions for Organization Theory

Organizations and Organization Theory

Managing with Power

Power in Organizations

The External Control of Organizations:
A Resource Dependence Perspective (with Gerald R. Salancik)

Organizational Design

7
RULES OF
POWER

Surprising—but True—
Advice on How to
Get Things Done and
Advance Your Career

JEFFREY PFEFFER

Matt Holt Books
An Imprint of BenBella Books, Inc.
Dallas, TX

Matt Holt is an imprint of BenBella Books, Inc.
10440 N. Central Expressway
Suite 800
Dallas, TX 75231
benbellabooks.com
Send feedback to feedback@benbellabooks.com

BenBella and *Matt Holt* are federally registered trademarks.

Printed in the United States of America
10 9 8 7 6 5 4 3 2 1

Library of Congress Control Number: 2021057134
ISBN 9781637741221 (cloth)
ISBN 9781637741238 (ebook)

Copyediting by James Fraleigh
Proofreading by Michael Fedison and Lisa Story
Indexing by WordCo
Text design and composition by PerfecType, Nashville, TN
Author photo by Toni Bird Photography
Cover design by Brigid Pearson
Printed by Lake Book Manufacturing

To the Amazing Kathleen, the Love of My Life,
Whose Death Left a Hole in My Heart & Soul

CONTENTS

IN THE BEGINNING
The Challenge of Power

*If you want power to be used for good, more good people
need to have power.*
—A quote attributed to me.

I REGULARLY SUFFER A FORM OF what might be called intellectual
whiplash. On the one hand, people—even a good friend and insightful editor—tell me my ideas about power don't fit the prevailing
zeitgeist with its emphasis on collaboration, being nice, and enact-
ing politically correct behavior. On the other hand, I get emails like
the one from an individual enrolled in my online class on power.
That person told me and his classmates that he learned that performance is not enough. Rather, he now knew he had to ask people in
power in his company for what he wanted and needed to advance
his career and achieve his job objectives and to flatter higher-ups; to
believe in himself and act and speak with power; to build a network
and support system; and, when confronting opposition and conflict,
to be smart in how and when to fight his battles. And oh, by the way,
he would miss my final live session because his network-building
and "get noticed" efforts had resulted in his being on the corporate

plane with two C-level officers to make an international market visit at the same time as the session.

So, what to believe about power? How to act—what to do? *7 Rules of Power* captures my current thinking and the most recent social science research to help you answer those questions.

| | |

WHY THIS BOOK, NOW?

I thought I would never write another book on power. I have written three,[1] four if you count a prequel[2] that confronts leadership aphorisms that are mostly untrue and unhelpful, like recommendations to be modest, authentic, and truthful. My last two books on power have done reasonably well, being used in classes literally worldwide; why this book, and why now?

Four things changed my mind. First, I have continued my efforts to convey material on organizational power and politics ever more effectively. I have the privilege of doing so for some of the most talented people in the world, both online and in person. This activity has deepened my insights about how to simplify, clarify, and articulate more clearly the ideas behind rules of power—how and why people can take actions that, very practically and often quickly, will alter their career trajectories and their lives.

Students have shown me how learning the rules of power and their application can have profoundly positive and immediate effects. A recent, not unusual email:

> *Thank you for all the lessons from your . . . class. It helped me start my own department, get a salary and title I never considered at my age, and today it got me praise from two ministers during an international signing ceremony. What's the secret? I simply asked for things. I also took your advice of strategically placing*

myself in places where my . . . degrees and AI knowledge are con-
sidered very rare instead of common. Lastly, I invested in putting
myself out there, networking with those at work, and building a
name for myself.

None of what this individual, a Saudi national working for
Aramco, described is rocket science, although all of what they did
is consistent with social science evidence—and all too infrequently
implemented. That this example comes from a different country and
culture suggests what research evidence says: the rules of power
are quite general and hold across cultures. Because of the positive
effects of this material, I thought I should share my expanding capa-
bility to teach about organizational power and, more broadly, my
most recent insights about helping people on their path to power.

The Magic Number Seven

After observing my former students as well as political and business leaders (particularly successful ones), and reviewing the relevant social science, I concluded that there were basically seven rules
of power. Organizing lessons about power into these seven fundamental rules is an effective way to teach people what they need to
do to have more influence and success.

Seven turns out to be a good number of rules. In 1956, George
Miller wrote an influential article arguing that "the unaided observer
is severely limited in the amount of information he can receive, process, and remember," with seven elements or ideas, plus or minus
two, constituting most people's capacity.[3] A more recent analysis of
Miller's argument noted that "the number 7 occurs in many aspects
of life, from the seven wonders of the world to the seven seas and
seven deadly sins."[4] Further research has consistently confirmed the
validity and robustness of Miller's original insight about cognitive
limitations once one gets much beyond seven items.

Fortunately, my ideas about the building and use of power can be effectively captured in seven rules, which constitute the chapters of this book. The seven rules are:

1. Get out of your own way.
2. Break the rules.
3. Appear powerful.
4. Build a powerful brand.
5. Network relentlessly.
6. Use your power.
7. Success excuses almost everything you may have done to acquire power.

I believe the seventh rule to be one of the more important, as it can cause people to act rather than worry needlessly about consequences.

Explaining the Current Leadership Landscape

The second factor that changed my mind was the observable reality of contemporary political and business leaders, including but certainly not limited to people like Donald Trump, Steve Jobs, Jeff Bezos, Bill Gates, Meg Whitman, Carly Fiorina, and Elon Musk, that I find people do not understand. Many people consider these individuals and their behaviors anomalies, but fail to recognize that as they exemplify the rules of power, these leaders offer important lessons about contemporary—yes, *contemporary*, not ancient— successful leadership behavior.

Trump surely follows the seven rules of power I outline in this book. In fact I originally intended to write about the leadership lessons of Trump. I decided against it because he is such a polarizing figure that people find it hard to objectively watch what he does and evaluate it outside the context of Trump himself. However, in thinking about why Trump has been so unexpectedly successful in politics and other domains, I developed insights into not only the social science foundations that help explain his success, but also the behavior and outcomes achieved by many other corporate leaders and politicians in the United States and elsewhere.

Because people do not understand the behavioral realities of power, they are continually surprised by both what happens and the effectiveness of actions that seemingly violate conventional wisdom about leadership—mostly because much of this wisdom is largely untethered from research on the social psychology of human behavior. Sometimes the surprise is accompanied by unanticipated career setbacks that arise because people are unprepared for the realities of social life.

My hope is that this book will help people better understand the everyday dynamics and political truths of organizations of all types, public and private. My explicit goal, stated in my Paths to Power course outline, is to provide people with the knowledge that, if implemented, can help them never have to leave a job involuntarily. Although I have not achieved that goal, as I still see too many people being ousted, the goal remains relevant and important. Teaching people how to put the seven rules of power into practice can help them achieve that objective.

Power Is Not a "Dark" Art; It's the Key to Success

My third motivation for writing this new book: all too frequently I encounter people, either by email or in my courses, who initially express resistance, skepticism, discomfort, challenges, and similar feelings with the ideas I teach. Not because they doubt the ideas' existence in the world or maybe even their validity founded on social science research or what they observe. To use the word of one recent email correspondent, they find the principles and research findings "depressing"—or, quoting my friend and colleague Bob Sutton, "dark." Consequently, people eschew opportunities to make things happen and accelerate their careers as effectively as they might.

I figured that one way to fight these perceptions was to provide people seven rules that, if they used them, would make them more powerful. Once people had more power, they would be much less depressed and experience the world as less dark, because they would be considerably more effective at getting things done as they navigated that world. They would also be physically and mentally healthier, because research shows that health is related to job control and one's position in the social hierarchy,[5] and happier, because power is associated with increased happiness.[6]

Have the Principles—the Rules—of Power Changed?

Fourth, I wanted to address directly the frequent narrative that today everything is different—fundamentally changed by new values, new generations (and their own new values), and new technologies, particularly social media—and therefore old ideas about power and influence are no longer relevant. That argument is why it is not surprising that people feel ambivalent about my class and writings, given the current attitude in business schools and other programs in leadership and administration. Power—and possibly even more so, organizational (or maybe all) politics—is on the outs.

Many books and research studies that are ostensibly about power are fundamentally ambivalent about embracing techniques to make people more powerful. Many commentaries on power, while optimistic and uplifting and often quite popular, are, in their Panglossian views of human behavior and the social world, remarkably untethered from the empirical realities of social life. By neglecting or actively rejecting the fundamental, enduring realities of power and human behavior, such commentators' earnest and well-meaning attempts to make things better—and different— are almost certainly doomed to fail, just as attempting to build a rocket without adhering to the laws of physics and thermodynamics is unlikely to succeed. Here are a few of the many examples of writings on power that I find disconnected from the data about actual power in the world.

Moses Naim wrote *The End of Power*,[7] about how powerful people in powerful roles are experiencing greater limits on their power. Naim notes how many people with fancy titles had confided in him about the perceived (or claimed) gaps between the power others attributed to them and both what they could get done and their own self-expressed perceptions of their power. When Mark Zuckerberg of Facebook fame launched a book club, he named this book his first selection.[8]

I trust you appreciate the irony. As I write this, Zuckerberg is recentralizing his control over Facebook, and of course Facebook, like many of its Silicon Valley peers, has a supermajority voting structure that assures, as *New York Times* technology columnist Kara Swisher has aptly noted, that Zuckerberg cannot be fired regardless of what he does.[9] Some people may face the end of power or limits on their power, but certainly not Zuckerberg; a lot fewer people have tenuous power than claim to.

In this same book, which I often hear about as an example of how theories and realities of power have fundamentally changed, Naim asks what globalization was doing to economic concentration. The presumption was that the globalization of business—and therefore, competition—would disperse economic power. He asked that question in 2013. By now the answer is clear, and it is not what many expected. Not only in the US but around the world, antitrust authorities are girding for battle because globalization has *increased* the concentration of power and wealth, particularly in technology multinationals but in other industries as well, such as telecommunications and even retail (perhaps you have heard of Amazon?). Following the 2008–2009 financial crisis, banks that were criticized as being too big to fail got—bigger. The story of nonexistent antitrust enforcement and increasing concentration of economic power is one often empirically told.[10]

Then there are Jeremy Heimans and Henry Timms, authors of *New Power*.[11] Their thesis is that power wasn't ending, but that power and its bases and use were being fundamentally transformed by things like the internet, social media, and new communication modalities. The result of this social and technological change was to be greater democratization, a word they use often, as the ideas of new power would make power less concentrated and available to more people. Their basic argument, expressed by numerous others, was that the ability of many individuals to readily acquire a communications platform (think blogs and accounts on social media platforms like Twitter, Facebook, and Instagram) and to easily access the world's information (think Google) would lead to a proliferation of innovation and social movements. Much like the oft-discussed but ultimately unsuccessful Arab Spring, there would be, to take a phrase from the 1960s, more power to the people, including those lacking formal positions of power.

Unfortunately, reality intruded, and the most successful users of the new communication methods and social media platforms turned out to be those who already held political and economic power. According to one Philippines-based observer of the media scene, "Power is consolidating power" almost everywhere in the world, as independent news groups are eliminated, enabling the voice "with the loudest megaphone" to shape reality.[12] *The Economist* Intelligence Unit, which since 2006 has compiled a democracy index, noted that "democracy is in retreat . . . The global score of 5.44 out of ten is the lowest recorded since the index began."[13] Or maybe you prefer the Human Freedom Index, published by the conservative Cato Institute since 2008. Since that time, overall freedom in the world has decreased, with 61 countries increasing their ratings and 79 decreasing.[14]

To take some examples of the consolidation of power from the political realm, in China, Xi Jinping has officially made himself ruler for life, as, in effect, has Russia's Vladimir Putin. Authoritarian rule is on the rise in numerous other European and Asian countries, including Hungary, Poland, Turkey, and the Philippines. Hong Kong's special status has mostly eroded with China increasingly circumscribing its rights. In the United States, Donald Trump won the presidency in 2016 first by effectively harnessing "new power communication modalities" such as Facebook, then—according to the fact checkers at the *Washington Post*—by telling numerous falsehoods,[15] with the Republican Party ultimately falling in line behind him. Although he (barely) lost reelection in 2020, Trump received the second most votes in the history of presidential elections, exceeding his 2016 tally.

In short, power is not ending, nor are many of its manifestations new. To effectively lead in a world that has not changed as much as many think or expect, people need to understand the basic principles—the rules—of power.

USING ANALYSIS AND DATA TO CREATE A MORE POWERFUL YOU

Maybe these facts and many like them are "depressing" or "dark." But to reprise the quote with which I opened this chapter, if power is to be used for good, more good people need power. And if they are going to get that power, they need to understand the well-established social science verities that will permit them to succeed in a world where power has neither disappeared, nor become less concentrated, nor changed in its determinants and strategies. Simply put, people need to embrace the rules of power, not run from them. My job in this book is not to make you happy or tell you stories that uplift your spirits. All the same, I consider myself not a cynic but a pragmatist and a realist.

Since 1979, I have taught as a full professor at Stanford University's Graduate School of Business. My course on power in organizations is one of the most popular electives, not because of my charm or charisma and certainly not because the material fits the prevailing ethos. It has succeeded because, as one student put it, "your class actually helps us understand the world we continually encounter," and does so in a way that makes many people demonstrably more effective and successful. The school's motto is "Change lives, change organizations, change the world." Change requires power. If change were going to happen without power and influence, it would have already. The first step to making change is to get yourself (and your allies) into positions of leverage—a word I am going to use a lot in this book—so that your efforts have disproportionate effects in accomplishing things. If you want happy talk, this is not the place for you.

My reading material reflects this mindset. Among the books sitting on my desk are one titled *How to Be a Dictator: The Cult of Personality in the Twentieth Century*, which won the Samuel Johnson Prize;[16] *Cheaters Always Win: The Story of America*;[17] and *Cheating*,[18] by my late Stanford law school colleague Deborah Rhode. All of them are worth reading for their deep understanding of the realities of history and human behavior. Their message: life is not always fair, even though people "cling to the idea that people generally get what they deserve."[19] People are seduced by and attracted to narcissists and despots and wind up voting for or working for them, frequently with bad outcomes. Honesty is not automatic or inevitable, but needs institutional structures and sanctions—unfortunately, often missing—to organize social life and reduce cheating and deception. You get the point.

Sociologist Murray Edelman wrote several books on political language. One has a line that I particularly appreciate.[20] Paraphrased, it goes: it is often the case in politics that one side gets the rhetoric, the other the reality. Despite all the talk about the changes in power dynamics, new power, the end of power, and so forth, much as magicians wave their hands so you aren't as likely to see their tricks, people are diverted from the fundamental understandings that can make them more successful and effective. If you read this book and follow its advice, you will *not* be one of those people.

I offer one other recommendation. When you hear people—leaders, academics, "gurus" (a term I detest)—provide advice and tell their stories, do a modicum of due diligence. You possess access, through online databases and other sources, to a wealth of information. Go online and see how many lawsuits have been filed against these people, what various websites say about their leadership styles. Better yet, track down those who have worked with and for these wonderful leaders and teachers, and talk to them about the realities of their organizations and behavior. Or seek out stories journalists have written about them. Simply put, engage in some critical thinking and investigate. You will soon see that, to paraphrase Shakespeare with the line "Methinks the lady doth protest too much" from *Hamlet*, often the people who most forcefully advocate authenticity and transparency are the least likely to possess those qualities. No, you don't need to believe me and the welter of social science evidence I will provide about the rules of power. You can believe your own eyes—as long as you bother to keep your eyes open.

INTRODUCTION
Power, Getting Things Done, and Career Success

On May 10, 2019, Rukaiyah Adams received the Tapestry Award from Stanford's Graduate School of Business. The award honors African American alumni "who have woven inspirational leadership, intellectual excellence, and service to others through their professional and personal life."[1] Today Adams is chief investment officer of the $750 million Meyer Memorial Trust, headquartered in Portland, Oregon. Previously she chaired the board that oversees $100 billion in public pensions and other assets for Oregon. A former student in my class who has a law degree as well as an MBA, Adams faced a horrible job market when she graduated in 2008 and had difficulty landing a suitable position. She was a Black woman in an industry (asset management) that had few African Americans or women; a recent study reported that of the $69.1 trillion in global financial assets, women and people of color managed less than 1.3 percent of them.[2] Adams quickly had to figure out how to turn what could have been a problem—being different—into a strength. She said, "Clearly these organizations are not going to impart power and opportunity on me, so I have to make it myself." She found a position at a hedge fund where she became a trusted confidante. Adams commented:

> What once was a position of an outsider, being black and female, became an information conduit. People told me things they wanted raised, but they were too fearful to raise themselves because they were so deeply invested in their need to support their families, and most of them had spouses who didn't work . . . I was young and single and as far as they were concerned, a total outsider already. They felt that they could tell me things and raise issues. Then the executive team began to pivot to me when they needed information . . . I was in a position of power. That turned into a promotion to the COO seat, and once I was in that seat, the investors turned to me to tell them the truth during really different times.

By 2012, Adams was managing six trading desks and $6.5 billion in assets for a Portland financial services company.

Rukaiyah Adams mastered the lessons from the class I teach. She understood the importance of being central in communication networks, a topic we will revisit when we look at the importance of networking in chapter five. Most importantly, she understood the first rule of power: to get out of her own way—to not expect a just or fair world, and certainly not to play by rules that would leave her disadvantaged, but instead to make her own rules and play her own game.

I would love to say that Adams's success was because of my class—which she mentioned in her award speech—but Adams graduated near the top of her MBA class and has two professional degrees. Power is seldom the most important source of success, but what it can do, as it did for Rukaiyah Adams, is help leverage your performance and talent. Job performance is important, but if no one notices that performance, it is for naught. Power and performance together will get you much further ahead than either one separately. Adams both embraced the principles of power and understood how she could use them to reach positions of influence, from which she could achieve both personal goals and her objective of advancing a set of social causes. She noted, "I think I was drawing on the kind of power that Black women have to improvise and survive."

Not everyone embraces the rules of power as Adams did. I well understand the psychological barriers some people confront in accepting material on power and, even more importantly, putting it into use. People typically go through various stages of resistance as they take the class—or for that matter, as they read my books on power. The purpose of this introductory chapter is to get you through any skepticism and resistance more quickly, so you can get on with your learning and, even more importantly, put it to use and improve your circumstances as much and as swiftly as possible.

POWER IS A TOOL PUT TO MANY USES

Most fundamentally, power is a tool. Like many or maybe most tools, power, once mastered, can be used to accomplish great things, horrendously terrible things, and everything in between. The point: Don't confuse or conflate your reactions to "power" with your reactions to how, or for what, it has been deployed—particularly if it has been deployed successfully against you. Don't resent the inevitable ubiquity of power in social life; instead, master it.

Here's one example (among many) of seeing power and then learning about its use, not evaluating it by its results. In 1985, the late John Jacobs,[3] then a Knight Journalism Fellow at Stanford for the year and a student in my class, and who later became the chief political reporter for the McClatchy newspapers, gave me a book that he had coauthored. The inscription inside: "To Jeff Pfeffer, who no doubt would appreciate this man's power base." The book: *Raven: The Untold Story of the Rev. Jim Jones and His People.*[4] Before leaving the US and inciting mass murder and suicide in Guyana, Jones had very effectively insinuated himself into the San Francisco political power structure by using many of the techniques I teach.

Jones cultivated a relationship—to cite Rule 5, he networked—with Dr. Carlton Goodlett, one of the more powerful African Americans in San Francisco, who published a newspaper that provided Jones favorable coverage. Jones sent presents to politicians and invited them to Peoples Temple events and dinners, thus activating the norm of reciprocity—a norm so powerful that people repay favors even if they know the favor-doer won't know if they reciprocated.[5] Jones had Peoples Temple members volunteer to work in the political campaign of soon-to-be mayor George Moscone and a liberal slate of candidates for the 1975 city election, and bundled contributions that supported the liberal takeover of city politics that year. Jones made sure the recipients knew where the money and volunteer labor hours were coming from, not simply relying on reciprocity, but also signaling to the politicians that Jones controlled valuable monetary and human resources, so they would be well served to have Jones on their side. After Moscone won, Jones asked for and received an appointment to the San Francisco Housing Authority, thereby obtaining an aura of legitimacy for him and his organization as he received favorable press coverage that helped him build a positive brand.[6]

Just because Jim Jones used many techniques found to be effective in acquiring power does not make those behaviors bad or wrong. Jones used them for malign purposes, but they can also be used for good. To be clear, my task in this book is to teach you as much as I can about the rules of power and how to use them. It is up to you to decide the ends or purposes to which you will apply this knowledge. This idea of teaching you the rules of power in a value-neutral way—much as one might teach about the physics of atomic energy—is a "different" approach from the one many colleagues take.

Several people in the leadership education business have decided that their real role is as lay preachers—to teach you ethics, values, and ideals, along with maybe some social science, particularly if that social science conforms to those ideals. They may decide to shield you from research on topics such as narcissism[7] or the frequency of lying and the absence of consequences for doing so[8] if they think such subject matter would be disturbing. This is a position I completely reject. Not that ideals, values, and so forth aren't important. Of course they are. But there are three problems with conflating "principles" (as in moral or ethical principles) with learning about the skills and tactics of leadership.

First, the evidence on whether even teaching ethical principles actually increases ethical behavior is decidedly mixed, notwithstanding research paradigms designed to find an effect, such as putting people into hypothetical situations or measuring their knowledge of appropriate behavior rather than their actual behaviors. For example, a matched-pairs study (where people are matched on important demographics and other characteristics and then one person is given the treatment—in this case some ethics training—and the other, the control, is not) of undergraduates at an Australian university concluded that "ethics education has limited impact on students' responses to ethical dilemmas."[9] A study of students' cheating behavior found no effect of education or training on actual cheating.[10] A review of the effect of teaching classes on business and society and business ethics concluded that any improvement "appears to be short-lived."[11] A reasonably comprehensive review of corporate-based ethics training noted that the evidence on its effectiveness was inconclusive. This article noted that "incorporating the principles of responsible management into training does not automatically lead to behavioral change among practicing professionals because cognitive growth alone does not produce the ability and readiness to act responsibly at work."[12]

Second, it is far from clear that anyone other than someone's family or clergy has the right—or even the obligation—to tell others what their goals and objectives in their lives should be. We can tell people what we know about individual and organizational behavior, and we can help them think through how to make decisions. But what people want to achieve with that knowledge is, in my view, up to them.

Third, there is the fundamental issue of the relationship between means and ends, a topic endlessly debated in philosophy.[13] If the goals are lofty and deserving, should there be constraints (and if so, what limits) on the tactics—the means—used to achieve those goals? Robert Moses, the "master builder" of New York City and one of the most powerful people of the twentieth century, someone who wielded enormous influence over the physical development of New York for four decades, famously said, "If the ends don't justify the means, what does?"[14] (You'll learn more about Moses in my discussion of Rule 2, "Break the Rules.")

One reason why people fail to achieve their objectives or lose out in competitions for high-status positions is their unwillingness to do what is required to prevail. In fact, the first rule of power, covered in the next chapter, is for people to get out of their own way, including the many constraints they impose on themselves that render them less effective. Deciding what means to employ in pursuing one's goals is a personal choice. But to make that choice, I believe you need to understand as much as possible about what works, and what doesn't, and why. And you also need to understand that some of your rivals may not have the same reluctance to go "all in" and to play the game to win.

DOES POLITICAL SKILL INFLUENCE CAREER OUTCOMES?

A woman from Nigeria who took the online version of my power class in a program called LEAD emailed me:

> The reason I applied to LEAD was because I felt totally power-less. I was alone as a woman in a male-dominated geoscience and engineering world. My former boss, 20 years older than me, practically bullied me day in and day out. It was a very difficult moment. When I started the doing power project and using the advice—not answering immediately, speaking with power [the

topic of chapter three], networking and building influence [she created nonprofit organizations that connect up-and-coming women and other young professionals], now he and all the other colleagues have lined up behind me. They respect me but the beautiful thing is that I don't need to worry about them any-more as I am now one-on-one with C-suite executives in my company. I live a stress-free life, running my own thing, helping others and shining my light around the world. I never thought that it was possible to live like this. Having power is a must. It changes the narrative.

Following the rules of power changed her life, in less than eight weeks. That's because power changes how others relate to people, often in a positive fashion, while providing its wielders with more autonomy and control over their lives. And because power makes people like my Nigerian student more independent and successful, it also makes them much happier.

Research shows that feeling powerful is associated with higher levels of subjective well-being. A study relating people's sense of power (e.g., "I think I have a great deal of power") to their satis-faction with life (e.g., "In most ways my life is close to my ideal") and to their positive and negative affect (i.e., their perceived mood and emotions) found that, even after gender and other personal-ity dimensions were statistically controlled, power predicted well-being.[15] "Participants with high . . . power were 16% more satisfied with their lives, and experienced 15% more PA [positive affect] and 10% less NA [negative affect], than participants with low . . . power."[16]

Of course, success (and, for that matter, happiness and wellbe-ing) means different things to different people. I cannot speak to any of that as I am not a moral philosopher, nor do I offer life advice or coaching. But as a social scientist, I—and you—can access the research literature and ask, with respect to specific measures that index aspects of career success, what seems to predict the attain-ment of those outcomes. To take this book about the rules of power seriously, the first and most fundamental questions have to be: Does possessing political skill in developing and wielding power actually matter? Do people who engage in power-relevant actions fare better?

Florida State professor Gerald Ferris and his colleagues have spent many years defining and measuring political skill and studying its effects on people and their careers. In a recent book summarizing their extensive research program, they defined political skill as "the ability to effectively understand others at work and to use that knowledge to influence others to act in ways that enhance one's personal and/or organizational objectives."[17] Political skill—mastering power dynamics—does affect careers, as ample research shows. As Ferris and his colleagues concluded, "Political skill is one of the most powerful predictors of success in the workplace."[18] Here is a small sampling of the extensive empirical evidence that shows why people should assiduously build their power skills.

An assessment of 191 people working in a wide range of occupations related political skill to five career outcomes—total compensation, promotions, career satisfaction, life satisfaction, and perceived external job mobility—and found that political skill was associated with four of them.[19] A study of elected employee representatives in German companies found that political skill was related to career attainment as assessed by success in upward elections.[20] A review of the performance of casework teams in a child welfare system found that the political skill of team leaders explained a significant fraction of the variation in team performance scores.[21] And a comprehensive meta-analysis—a summary of multiple study results—of the effects of political skill found that it was positively related to job satisfaction, work productivity, career success, and personal reputation, and negatively related to physiological strain.[22] Together these studies confirm Ferris and colleagues' assertion that political skill directly affects career success.

Another way that political skill affects career outcomes is by making people more effective at using other tools of influence more skillfully. For instance, political skill helps people develop and use network resources,[23] makes them more effective at using various impression-management techniques,[24] helps them ingratiate themselves with their bosses,[25] and (in Chinese firms) improves supervisor–subordinate *guanxi* (the system of social networks and influential relationships that facilitate business and other dealings) and therefore career prospects.[26] Political skill also reduces the adverse effects of workplace stressors;[27] experiencing less stress helps people get things done by giving them more energy and permitting them to focus better. Networking, flattery/ingratiation, creating a positive impression by displaying confidence—these and many other influence techniques require skill to get the best results. Having more political skill also improves people's ability to deploy other influence skills.

University of California, Berkeley business school professor Cameron Anderson and some colleagues conducted a longitudinal study (in which researchers collect several observations of the same respondents over time) of 214 alumni from their universities. People's self-rated power and their power as assessed by others in their organization was the dependent variable—the two measures of power were highly correlated. The study found that the attainment of power was associated with more behavior that was dominant-aggressive, political, communal behavior, and competent. Of the four forms of behavior, political behavior had the strongest effect in their study, followed closely by competent behavior.[28]

Thus, the answer from a wealth of empirical research seems clear: political skill and engaging in political behaviors matter—a lot. On reflection, these effects on job and life satisfaction, as well as salary and position, are not surprising. People are going to enjoy more positive affect to the extent that they have more status, power, and success.

THE STAGES OF LEARNING ABOUT POWER

I have found that notwithstanding the ample social science evidence consistent with the material I teach and write about, and people's own observations from their lived experience, including the news, they often go through a series of stages as they learn about power. The first stage is denial. Because many of the principles of power diverge—sometimes quite a bit—from what people may have read or heard elsewhere about power, or what they learned from their families, or what various institutions, including even business schools, have inculcated in them, their first reaction will be to try and deny the validity of the ideas. Denial occurs even though (or maybe particularly because) people have seen and will keep seeing manifestations of power and political behavior in their daily lives.

Denial most often takes the form of finding a counterexample of some successful person who did not follow the seven rules of power. First of all, a single counterexample doesn't prove anything. There are people who spontaneously recover from life-threatening cancers, but that does not make relying on such remission an optimal strategy. Second, many of the people offered as counterexamples are excellent at creating a compelling personal narrative and promulgating it widely and repeatedly. Under this scrutiny, some of the counterexamples fall apart.

Denial also takes the form of saying these principles are not applicable in contemporary life because the rise of social media or new generations have changed the rules of power. Denial has people telling me that the rules of power don't apply in different national cultures—for instance, in Asia—or are not relevant in small companies, or high-technology fields, or partnerships. Denial takes many forms. Yet sometimes denying the ubiquity of power in organizational life has bad consequences.

Some years ago, as I shopped at the Safeway store in Burlingame near where I live, a voice behind me called out, "Professor Pfeffer." A former student from my class said hello and told me that the class had been very useful—in convincing him that he was unwilling to do what I was teaching. So, he said, he had formed an investment partnership with some classmates, where power and politics were at a minimum. "Good for you," I replied. Understanding the paths to power could certainly lead people to conclude that they did not want to go down those paths.

A few years later, by coincidence, I ran into the same student at the same Safeway. I said hello and reminded him of our conversation from our last encounter. How were things going with his small investment firm, I inquired. With a sort of twisted smile, he said that he was no longer with the firm—his partners had thrown him out. He explained that he could not escape the realities of power politics even in a small firm that he had cofounded. For him, the denial was over, albeit at a cost.

Denial is often followed by anger—frequently directed at me. That is not surprising. There is a large literature on the phenomenon of "killing the messenger"—just look at what happens to most whistleblowers, even when they turn out to be correct.[29] People do not want to hear what they don't want to hear, and few will thank you for telling them unpleasant facts. So people wonder, *how can I teach such terrible, difficult ideas, so different from what so much of the conventional leadership literature espouses?*

Anger typically passes, usually followed by sadness. Recognizing that the power principles are true, that I actually do know the social science research literature and understand some things about organizational behavior, people become unhappy. They do not like what I teach implies about the world in which they live and the implications for their own behavior and what they need to do. Who can they trust? Must they be constantly on guard and vigilant? That's when I hear the word "depressing."

If I am successful, which of course I am not always, sadness gives way to acceptance. People come not only to recognize what they need to do to change lives, organizations, and the world, they understand that they only have the choice of leaning into the rules of power and using them, or opting out, with all that the idea of opting out implies. Fortunately, I have been privileged over the years to see many of our graduates and other people accept the ideas of power, then do remarkable things.

Become Less Judgmental

Here's a hint about how to get to the acceptance stage of power more quickly and easily: become less judgmental.

Implementing this recommendation will require substantial effort. We live in a world where we are continually asked to render judgments—ratings—about products and experiences, getting us in the habit of judging. Yet many of these judgments turn out to be wrong. For instance, there is only a very small correlation between student ratings of teachers and objective measures of student learning. Moreover, what association there exists is situational, and not applicable to all teachers, disciplines, or levels of instruction. "The more objectively learning is measured, the less likely it is to be related to the evaluations."[30] Another example: A study of 1,272 products found that average user ratings do not agree with *Consumer Reports* scores.[31] One reason to become less judgmental is that our judgments are often neither accurate nor helpful.

Nonetheless, extensive evidence from social psychology indicates that "many day-to-day impressions and judgments of others occur rapidly, unwittingly, and intuitively. A fleeting glimpse or a mere glance can lead to an instantaneous evaluating judgment. Once made, such judgments provide the anchor from which subsequent judgments are realized."[32] People form judgments of others in about ten seconds, judgments that then prove remarkably stable. So, becoming less judgmental requires serious effort.

Two problems arise from making judgments of others. First, to get things done, critical relationships need to work. This fact is particularly true in organizational contexts, which are invariably characterized by interdependence—the fact that your ability to get things done depends importantly on others' actions. Once someone has formed a negative judgment of another—about their competence, morality, deservingness of the position they hold, and so forth—it is difficult to completely hide the content of that judgment. And if it is a negative judgment, that makes forming a positive relationship with the other person to accomplish an interdependent task less likely. "Our judgments interfere with many of our relationships."[33]

Second, judgment is a source of unhappiness and discontent, because in comparing what is with what we think should be, the almost inevitable observed discrepancies lead to frustration and negative affect. That is why there are many recommendations to be less judgmental. Mother Teresa famously said, "If you judge people, you have no time to love them."[34] The American poet Walt Whitman advised, "Be curious, not judgmental."[35]

The reality television program *MasterChef Australia* thought it had a coup when it got His Holiness, the Dalai Lama, to agree to appear as a guest judge. However, "he refused to render judgments: 'As a Buddhist monk it is not right to prefer this food or that food,' he said . . . There is a 6th-century Chinese text of the Chan (Zen) school that says: 'To set up what you like against what you dislike is a disease of the mind.' Very simply, sorting all phenomena into 'like' or 'dislike' bins gets in the way of enlightenment."[36] Likewise, in the New Testament, Matthew 7:1 says, "Judge not, that ye be not judged."

Judgment gets in the way of building helpful interpersonal relationships and sets us up for unhappiness, which is why eschewing judgment is so frequently recommended. Making judgments about power and its occurrence in organizational contexts has the same consequences, often rendering people less effective in navigating the interpersonal environment and leaving them feeling distressed by the realities of organizational life. Much better to be less judgmental and instead work from a place of equanimity, accepting (or at least understanding) organizational power and politics while becoming much more psychologically prepared to deal with them.

DO THESE RULES OF POWER ONLY APPLY TO WHITE MEN?

Civil rights laws and numerous social initiatives notwithstanding, ample evidence shows that gender- and race-based career discrimination persists. Moreover, people of color and women confront normative expectations for how they are supposed to behave that often vary starkly from the rules of power outlined in this book. Specifically, women and minorities are expected to follow the rules, not break them as I advise in chapter two, and frequently have been socialized to work for the welfare of the collective rather than engaging in activities such as brand building (chapter four) and networking (chapter five), which are seen as more individualistic and self-promoting. These expectations for what people are *supposed* to do and how they are supposed to be raises a question I get all the time: Do the power principles—the rules—work for women and minorities, too?

I have several responses to this important question. First, in considering research findings, it is important to choose the appropriate comparison. Many of the rules and strategies of power are undoubtedly less effective for women than for men, for instance. But the question is not, to take one example, whether using powerful language and projecting a powerful appearance is less effective for women or people of color. The question should be, is using powerful language and projecting power better than doing the opposite? Since people are not going to change their race or gender, the issue becomes, given who they are, how they can be as effective as possible in gaining power and influence. Regarding the specific example of projecting power through body language, Berkeley business school faculty member and nonverbal-behavior expert Dana Carney notes that there is not much evidence to suggest that the various ways of nonverbally expressing power, status, and social dominance are less effective for women than for men.[37]

Second, as I argued in an article about why power principles tended to persist both over time and across cultures, many aspects of power are unchanging.[38] Most organizations and social situations have hierarchical elements; as there are fewer positions at the top than at the bottom, competition is almost inevitable. The dimensions of interpersonal judgments—warmth and competence—also hold across cultures. People prefer similar others, and for reasons of self-enhancement, also favor associating themselves—forming alliances—with others who they believe will be successful and powerful. These social constants should frame how everyone thinks about strategies for building influence.

Third, many former students, including women and people of color, have told me that the rules of power are actually more important for them, and that understanding power dynamics has helped them to succeed. To take one out of many examples, consider Tadia James, a Black woman who worked for a venture capital firm before forming her own company. Recall from earlier in this chapter how people of color and women manage under 1.3 percent of the world's $69.1 trillion in financial assets.[39] James and I talked about how and why she recommends my last power book to everyone, and then we discussed the pushback the class and book receive, particularly about the general applicability of the material. She commented:

> There was a lot of pushback in the class, because people felt like, "Oh, these rules don't work if you are a person of color. They don't work if you're a woman." That just wasn't my experience at all. Understanding how to go around the rules, understanding how to build rapport with people that makes them want to engage with you, all of those things are really important in terms of building your career professionally. I think it's easier for people to say that doesn't apply to me than to do the work that sometimes can be uncomfortable to get the power that they need to get stuff done. I think it's easier for people to say, "that doesn't work for me" than

to actually put it into practice because it makes them feel better about themselves. Because if they knew that they could use these tactics and that they work, then there's nothing that they can complain about because they have the knowledge.

An executive coach who works with both my online and on-campus classes and who is actively engaged with Stanford's women in management group, Inbal Demri talks about reframing. She phrases it this way: building power and influence requires qualities and skills that can be learned and developed. The playing field is *not even* and on many issues, women, for instance, get the short end of the stick. But then she goes on to ask: Are you using this as an excuse or as information? Her primary point is about the importance of reframing, for instance, in the domain of gendered expectations. For example, Demri notes that women are expected to be communal in their networking behavior. Her reframe: Be strategic about relationships and ensure reciprocity, and recognize that women need different types of networks. Or on the topic of visibility, being an "only" or one of a very few makes you stand out. All right, says Demri: leverage that visibility, that difference, to your advantage. A third example: Women are expected to be helpful, to advocate for others and for the greater good. Demri's reframe: Remember to ask for things for yourself as well, and don't forget about your own interests and agenda, because if you do not advocate for yourself, others may not push for your interests, either.

Inbal Demri's fundamental point, one that I hear from many successful women and people of color: people can use the fact that the world is not fair and that many things are stacked against them as an excuse to opt out and not try to build power. But that gets them nowhere. People need to understand the obstacles they face because of their race, gender, social class, and so forth, but then they need to master the power skills and rules to improve their prospects. Or as Alison Davis-Blake, the first female dean at the University of Minnesota business school, and then the first female dean at the University of Michigan's Ross School of Business before becoming president of Bentley University, would tell my class: "Women need to be twice as good to get half the credit. Fortunately many women are four times as good."

Of course, adapt your implementation of the rules of power to your specific style and circumstances. But use them, because they do indeed work.

|R|U|L|E|

1

Get Out of Your Own Way

SITTING IN MY OFFICE IS CHRISTINE, a former student from my class on power who did management consulting at one of the fancy firms before returning to business school. Now working for a prestigious Silicon Valley company in a marketing analytics role, she had recently completed a project that had a $4 million economic impact. The problem: She was one of four peers, and one of them had gone to their mutual boss with the suggestion that Christine and her group report to him. A smart move, because not only would he have downgraded a competitor, he could take credit for her group's continuing outstanding work.

Christine, a woman of Asian origin, had been raised by her family to be polite, deferential, and to succeed on the basis of merit—hard work and good results. She tells me that before coming to see me to figure out a "paths to power" approach to her problem, as she called it, she tried a very different intervention. One of the most popular classes at Stanford's business school, interpersonal dynamics—nicknamed "touchy-feely"—is a sensitivity training–based class that helps students build their interpersonal relationship skills as they become aware of how others see them.

I ask what the relevance of that class was to her situation. Her reply: the material in the course teaches people skills and techniques for understanding themselves and others and repairing relationships that have soured. How did that work? Not well, because her peer/competitor was not interested in building a positive relationship or repairing the interpersonal friction. Instead he was pursuing his agenda to get Christine's group to report to him, so he could advance his career. She wants to know what she should do.

Before we strategize, I note that in our brief conversation, Christine has mentioned several times that she is the only woman in the setting (her three peers and boss are all men), is the youngest, and has the least seniority in the company. I am sure that is all true, because we are discussing observable demographics, but, I say, let me give you three other adjectives that describe you. You are the only one of this group with an MBA from a prestigious business school, the most analytically skilled, and the person who has run the project with the greatest economic impact. She sits up a little straighter and agrees. So, I say, we have six adjectives to describe you, three that imply you are not as deserving, and three that enhance your status. You get to pick which three you want to carry around in your head. How people think of themselves invariably influences what they project to others and what behaviors they will enact. The lesson: use self-descriptive adjectives that convey power, and eschew attitudes that, even if accurate, fairly or unfairly, diminish your status.

Christine won her power struggle—how is not important—and soon thereafter moved to another company. Then, when her sponsor at the new company lost a power struggle and left, she moved to a business where her analytical skills were even more valued and that went public at what is today a huge valuation. Her movement along a path to more influence had to begin not with a series of tactics—although those were important—but most fundamentally with a sense of herself that permitted her to engage in the political contests that are often part of organizational life, and to do so with a sense of her own empowerment and deservingness.

I cannot begin to tell you how typical this story is. Talented people, with objectively amazing accomplishments, hold self-descriptions that disempower themselves and that, if and when internalized, inappropriately limit their career prospects. Powerful, accomplished, successful people tell their stories in ways that downplay their gifts and accomplishments. Such behavior is unhelpful.

Many people, particularly in professional settings such as nursing, medicine, and academia, either as faculty or (doctoral) students—particularly those from groups that have been discriminated against, such as women or first-generation college students—suffer from what the research literature calls imposter syndrome. "*Imposter syndrome* is a psychological term that refers to a pattern of behavior wherein people (even those with adequate external evidence of success) doubt their abilities and have a persistent fear of being exposed as a fraud."[1] Imposter syndrome was first described in 1978, and research into the phenomenon has proliferated recently. Evidence shows that it affects as many as two out of three people in certain settings. Importantly, imposter syndrome can lead to a cycle of self-defeating behavior. "As part of a vicious cycle . . . imposters feel more prone to failure, may become less productive, and are characterized by insecurity and procrastination."[2]

In a class session on personal branding, a woman with a degree in medicine, accomplished enough to have been admitted to Stanford, told a compelling story about the product and company she was working on and how it related to her own history. Afterward, she confided to me that she was so nervous that her heart was racing when she faced the class. People tend to respond more positively to confidence than to doubt, but sometimes nervousness "leaks." Moreover, with enough imposter syndrome, people will be reluctant to pitch their ideas, or themselves, in the first place. Imposter syndrome is both real and very important for determining people's success.

One way of getting over imposter syndrome is to focus on others in high-level positions and their differences from you, if any. Many of them are no more qualified than you are; success is sometimes the result of luck or being born to the right parents. Another way to move past imposter syndrome is to do what this woman and other people sometimes do: push or force themselves, even in situations where they are uncomfortable, to present and sell themselves. With experience comes more comfort as well as skill. Getting over imposter syndrome is a first step on a person's path to power.

Mastering imposter syndrome, and describing yourself in positive rather than self-deprecating ways, is critical for achieving power and success. If you do not think of yourself as powerful, competent, and deserving, it is likely that, in subtle and possibly not-so-subtle ways, you will communicate this self-assessment to others. Others are not likely to think more favorably of you than you do of yourself. Colleagues expect that you will, at least to some extent, self-advocate and self-promote—and if you don't, that behavior will be held against you. In a paper I coauthored with the famous social psychologist Robert Cialdini, we wrote, "There is evidence that not to make positive assertions about oneself or one's work can be taken as a negative signal."[3] So, if you do not project power and confidence, and your self-description is limited in its ambitions and claims, your social status and career will suffer. (I more thoroughly explore the importance of body language and voice for projecting power in chapter three.)

Here's a practical exercise that you can do and then repeat occasionally as part of your personal development. Write down the adjectives you use to describe yourself, both to yourself and to others. Check with friends to see if your list is correct. Then ask yourself what descriptors you need to get rid of in order to project yourself in a more powerful way. Ask yourself what positive adjectives about yourself—language that gives credit to your accomplishments and credentials—you underutilize in your interactions with others.

A related exercise: record yourself as you interact in professional settings throughout a day or week. Then analyze how many times you begin an interaction by apologizing for intruding, for interrupting, for taking the other person's time, for offering your ideas. Ask friends and colleagues how often you actively participate in discussion and forcefully offer your opinions, and how often you begin interactions by apologizing for offering them.

And here's a third exercise you can and should do. As you describe yourself to others, as you articulate a narrative of your career so far, as you create a personal brand—a topic we will explore in more detail in Rule 4—do you talk about your accomplishments, your credentials, or what you have done successfully? Or do you attempt to appear modest and self-effacing, downplay your achievements, positions you have held, honors you have achieved, and your talents?

Using these exercises, figure out how you are going to change your self-image and self-presentation in ways that reduce how frequently you get in your own way by being too modest and thereby hinder your ability to project—and achieve—power. Change your behavior, and your attitudes about yourself and your place in the world quite likely will follow. That is because self-perception theory posits that "individuals come to 'know' their own attitudes, emotions, and other internal states partially by inferring them from observations of their own overt behavior."[4] People figure out what their attitudes are from the information available to them when they describe their attitude, and salient information about their own behavior, therefore, comes to influence their beliefs and attitudes.[5] Consequently, an individual can increase their confidence by acting more confidently, and can build their sense of their own power by describing themselves in a more powerful fashion.

People often worry about their organizational competitors for advancement, about what their bosses think of them, about their relative skills. All of these things are important. But possibly the single biggest barrier to having power is ourselves. Therefore, the first rule of power is to get out of your own way.

It is possible to do so. For example, at Stanford, we grade in part on class participation. Invariably at the start of the quarter, a few people will come to me and tell me that they are uncomfortable participating in class discussions. They are shy. They don't think they can add much to the discussion. They are not as articulate as some of their peers. English isn't their first language. The list goes on. My reply is always the same: much of social life, and certainly much of organizational life, is enacted through conversation. There is a field of sociological study called conversation analysis. A former post-doctoral fellow who worked with me at Stanford, the late Deidre Boden, wrote a book about language and conversation in business.[6] My point: if students are going to live up to their vast intellectual potential, they need to be able to hold their own in the conversations that constitute organizational life. My classroom is a relatively low-risk place for them to begin doing just that. Many times, at the end of the quarter, people have participated much more, and with more passion and energy, than they ever thought they could. Notwithstanding the results achieved over a brief ten weeks, even the effort to participate, to stand out, is worthwhile.

Changing the Narrative About Oneself

In the winter quarter of 2020, I was privileged to meet Christina Troitino in my class. She did some amazing things, two of which I will describe in the next chapter on rule breaking. Her family lives mostly in Venezuela, so she has seen some difficult circumstances. I asked her about her personal journey to getting out of her own way and how she became as bold as she is, because she has done some truly bold things. This is what she told me:

I always have thought of myself as shameless. I was very disenfranchised in my first job out of college. I worked at Amazon and I saw immediately that those who were the most capable are not necessarily always those who are in power. I was on the team at Amazon that got profiled by the New York Times *for mismanagement. It also became clear to me that for people my age, the traditional path of staying with the company, rising through the ranks, and all that sort of stuff was not the way people were becoming powerful. And beyond that, I'm Hispanic, co-president of the Hispanic Business Student Association. That, and being a female, being a minority in tech, it became very obvious to me that I would have to play the game very differently to get equal amounts of power as anyone else who was in a more privileged position.*[7]

Christina has indeed played the game very differently, as I describe in more detail in the next chapter. Her story illustrates two important points. First, experience taught her that the world was not always just and fair, so she needed to look out for herself. That is a lesson for everyone, even people of privilege, let alone women and people of color. Second, Christina demonstrated a great degree of self-awareness, both about the obstacles she would face and how, in doing so, those obstacles would force her to play the game differently if she wanted to be successful—a theme we will see again throughout the book and particularly in the next chapter on rule breaking. Self-awareness of where you sit in the ecosystem and what you need to do to win is something everyone would do well to develop.

BE WILLING TO DO WHATEVER IT TAKES— DON'T RUN AWAY FROM POWER

Everyone gets to determine what they are willing to do to acquire power, or even if they want it. I have had numerous people say to me over the years that if they had to play politics, or flatter their boss, or build interpersonal relationships for strategic purposes, or spend time promoting their accomplishments to become more influential, it would not be worth it. After all, as Harvard Business School professor Rosabeth Moss Kanter wrote in 1979, "Power is America's last dirty word . . . People who have it deny it; people who want it do not want to appear to hunger for it; and people who engage in its machinations do so secretly."[8]

People who see power as evil or dirty may abjure power and be unwilling to "play the game." A very positive review of my colleague Deborah Gruenfeld's excellent book, *Acting with Power*,[9] summed up a feeling I hear from many people: "I grew up in communist Poland where our leaders used power to advance their own interests so power was nothing I aspired to have or use. For me, it was a tool those higher up used to coerce others to do what they wanted."[10] Having observed power being used for self-advancement or in ways that hurt others, people opt out of the quest for power. But people who do not seek power pay a cost: as I noted in the Introduction, political skill is related to multiple measures of career success and happiness.

To try and get people to be at least somewhat more flexible and strategic in their thinking, I assign my class an article on US men's soccer that asks the interesting question: Does the team put itself at a disadvantage because it is bad at—and refuses to engage in—playacting by exaggerating contact to draw a foul? Describing the behavior of many other teams, a *New York Times* article noted, "For better or worse, gamesmanship and embellishment—or depending on your sensibilities, cheating—are part of high-level soccer. Players exaggerate contact. They amplify the mundane. They turn niggling knocks into something closer to grim death."[11] By so doing, soccer players draw fouls, get free kicks, and knock opponents out of the game on penalties—thereby increasing their odds of winning. The article lists the prominent stars, including Cristiano Ronaldo and Luis Suárez, who "regularly fall to the ground, particularly if they feel that they are going to lose possession. And why not? If it works, they get a free kick. If it doesn't, they were going to give up the ball anyway." In the book *Soccernomics*, Simon Kuper wrote, "The long refusal of English players to dive may have been an admirable cultural norm but they might have won more games if they had learned from Continental Europeans how to buy the odd penalty."

What is true in soccer—or in basketball, where drawing a foul is more common and much less frowned upon—is true in organizational life. Different people are willing to do different things in order to succeed. Just because you won't network, or flatter, or self-promote, certainly does not mean that all of your competitors will be as circumspect. To the extent people opt out of doing things their colleagues are willing to do—tactics that build power—they put themselves at a disadvantage.

The fundamental point: everyone has choices, not only about how they think of themselves, but about what they are willing or unwilling to do in the contest for power. You can opt in, or out. You can self-handicap, or, like Christina Troitino, "play the game very differently."

The Importance of Persistence and Resilience

An important part of being "willing to do what it takes" is sticking with efforts to build power and get things done in the face of opposition, criticism, obstacles, setbacks, and failures. Almost everyone, at some point in their lives and careers, will run into seemingly insurmountable obstacles and determined opponents who may unfairly deprecate others and spread misinformation about rivals. Because these difficulties are inevitable, I believe that persistence and resilience—sticking with things, while being sensible and changing strategies or approaches as necessary—frequently determine whether people will succeed in their rise to power.

Some examples of persistence and resilience: Willie Brown, the longest-serving speaker in the California Assembly and still, in his eighties, one of the most powerful politicians in the state, lost the election the first time he ran for the Assembly from a district in San Francisco, and lost the first time he ran to be speaker. Arthur Blank and Bernard Marcus cofounded Home Depot after getting fired from Handy Dan, a home improvement company.[12] Netflix CEO Reed Hastings's earlier experience founding and leading a software company, Pure Software, was decidedly mixed. Hastings has said he felt like a failure because of some of his decisions and twice asked Pure's board of directors to find a new CEO for the company.[13] My academic career began at the College of Commerce and Business Administration at the University of Illinois in Urbana–Champaign because I had been rejected by many higher-prestige departments, and the business administration department head at the time, marketing scholar Jagdish Sheth, decided to build the department by hiring people who were different from the mainstream. Eight years later, I was a full professor at Stanford on the basis of my thesis research, resource dependence theory,[14] which had been panned when I was initially on the market.

Safi Bahcall's book, *Loonshots,* has an interesting subtitle: *How to Nurture the Crazy Ideas That Win Wars, Cure Diseases, and Transform Industries.* Crazy ideas, not surprisingly, often don't work at first and also can generate enormous opposition. One of the stories Bahcall relates is that of Judah Folkman, who, had he lived, would have almost certainly won the Nobel Prize for medicine. Folkman was a pediatric surgeon working at Boston Children's Hospital. Bahcall wrote:

> *In 1971, Folkman had proposed that cancer cells interact with their hosts, sending out signals that trick surrounding tissues into preparing the local environment for a tumor to grow . . . His idea was to design a new kind of drug, one that blocks those signals and destroys those pipes. In other words, a drug that starves a tumor . . . For three decades, there was roughly a seven-year cycle between embarrassing deaths and spectacular rebirths of Folkman's idea . . . On June 1, 2003 . . . 32 years after Folkman*

*first proposed a new type of cancer therapy . . . an oncologist from
Duke University unveiled new results from a drug called Avastin . . . Avastin demonstrated the best results ever seen for pro-
longing survival in patients with colon cancer . . . It was instantly
clear that the drug and Folkman's ideas would transform the
treatment of cancer . . . Later, Folkman would say, "You can tell a
leader by counting the number of arrows in his ass."*[15]

If you want power, you need to toughen up and become able
to persist in the face of opposition and persevere even when confronted by setbacks. Persistence and resilience seem to require not
overly obsessing about what others think and say while possessing
enough ego strength to keep problems and criticism from throwing
you off course. Like other personal qualities that help make people
powerful,[16] persistence and resilience can be developed, particularly with practice, experience, and social support.

HOW LOW POWER PERPETUATES ITSELF

Several psychological processes perpetuate one's staying in a low-
power position. Like everything else I am writing about, people can
surmount these barriers.

About seven or eight years ago I met a doctoral student, Peter
Belmi, with whom I have subsequently done research. Belmi, of Fili-
pino descent from a self-described lower-class background, was my
Paths to Power course assistant for two years. As he recently told
me, the class opened his eyes. Although he has done research on a
number of topics, Belmi's primary research focus has been on how
status and power reproduce themselves psychologically—as distinct from how class and power reproduce structurally. Obviously
one way that status gets reproduced is through inheritance and the
many educational and other advantages people from upper-class
backgrounds enjoy. Belmi wanted to understand the psychological
processes that leave people trapped and unable to achieve upward

mobility. He believed that different social classes have different social and behavioral norms, some of which hamper lower-class people in their careers.

Through seven studies, Belmi (who now teaches at the University of Virginia) and University of British Columbia social psychologist Kristin Laurin tested the idea that there were class-based differences in the propensity to seek positions of power and in the strategies people were willing to use to attain power.[17] Belmi and Laurin identified two prototypical ways of achieving power. One is through behaving in a prosocial fashion such as working hard, helping coworkers, and striving in other ways on behalf of the collective good. The other is through politics—basically what I teach—which entails behaving strategically, flattering higher-ups, building helpful social relationships, and promoting one's accomplishments (the subject of chapter four, taking credit as you build a strong personal brand). They found no difference by class in people's beliefs about the *usefulness* of the two strategies—all people, regardless of their social origins, generally believed that both approaches were helpful. However, they uncovered class differences in people's willingness to actually use the two strategies, with people from lower social-class origins being much less willing to use political strategies.

In one interesting test of their ideas, Belmi and Laurin presented Stanford MBAs, during their first week in the program (to avoid as much social influence and contagion as possible), with the actual descriptions of seven second-year organizational behavior electives, including Paths to Power, on a questionnaire that gauged their interest in the courses while also measuring students' perceived childhood social-class rank. They found there was no effect of social class on students' propensity to express interest in any of the second-year electives except one. As predicted, not only were a higher proportion of MBAs interested in Paths to Power, but this was also the only course for which childhood social-class rank affected expressed preference.

Peter Belmi believes that one (but not the only) reason social class predicts willingness to use political-power-seeking behaviors is that there is considerable evidence that lower social class is associated with a more collective versus an individualistic orientation. This difference means that people from lower-class origins are less likely to be comfortable with doing things that they see as just furthering their own interests. In one of their studies, Belmi and Laurin found that there was no difference in people's interest in seeking positions of power when they could achieve those positions through prosocial means. This implies that there are not class differences in the desire for higher positions, only in the willingness to use political strategies to achieve them. Following up on the insight on class differences in individualism, Belmi and Laurin found that when they couched the quest for power in terms of being able to achieve a superordinate goal of helping others, the differences among social classes in their willingness to use political strategies disappeared.

I have incorporated this insight into my teaching. I have found that people are much more willing to engage with and embrace political strategies and concepts when they are presented in the context of a case of someone using them for the benefit of others.

In another study, Belmi and his colleagues found that social class helped predict people's overconfidence. Not surprisingly, people from higher-social-class backgrounds have a stronger and more positive sense of self, which leads them to exhibit more confidence—and even overconfidence—in their behavior. Because overconfidence can confer advantages in how others perceive people, a topic explored in more detail when we examine Rule 3 (showing up in a powerful fashion), one way in which social class differences perpetuate is through the mechanism of overconfidence. Research demonstrates that overconfidence causes people to appear more competent,[18] and this perception of greater competence then causes overconfident individuals to enjoy advantages in the eyes of others.[19]

Social class is also associated with differences in norms that govern power-relevant behavior. There are numerous examples of this phenomenon; one of my favorites comes from an article in the *Guardian* that is both an interview with the Ugandan-born author and musician Musa Okwonga and an extract from his recent book, *One of Them: An Eton College Memoir.*[20] The book describes Okwonga's experience at Eton, a place filled with upper-class individuals who had a sense that they were born to rule, and acted accordingly.

> *Boys . . . belong to a class that everyone refers to as "the lads," and they seem exempt from generally accepted codes of behaviour . . . I have been told my entire life that it is important to get on with people in order to succeed, but these peers of mine often seem supremely uninterested in that . . . I think a great deal about the English concept of fair play . . . The older I get, the more I wonder how much that concept was created to keep people of a certain social class in their place. I look at the most confident people in my year and I realise that the greatest gift that has been bestowed on them is that of shamelessness. Shamelessness is the superpower of a certain section of the English upper classes . . . The upper classes calmly parade on through the streets and boardrooms to claim the spoils. They don't learn shamelessness at Eton, but this is where they perfect it.*[21]

A woman friend who went to a comparable girls' school in the UK told me that the phenomenon Okwonga described was similar across genders. In her experience, the women, too, learned and perfected the shamelessness that permitted them to present themselves and do things that conveyed and built power.

Social class is not the only dimension that distinguishes groups in their willingness to use "political" strategies or their success in doing so. When Buck Gee and Wes Hom, two successful retired technology executives, sought to do something about the fact that Asian-background executives were well represented in lower ranks in the Silicon Valley (and elsewhere) but seldom made it to the top, they began quantifying the disparities. In one early report published by the Ascend Foundation, the data showed that race was 3.7 times as significant as gender in affecting a glass ceiling. That report also noted that "while white men are 42% more likely than white women to be an executive . . . they are 149% more likely than Asian men to be an executive, and 260% more likely than Asian women."[22]

When Gee and Hom organized an executive program with Stanford business school to see if they could accelerate Asians' and Asian-Americans' careers, among the topics they included from the beginning were two sessions drawn from my Paths to Power class. These were probably the most shocking—but also the most useful—sessions during the week, as they caused executives who believed in a just world and the ultimate triumph of merit to consider the possibility of expanding their repertoire to include some power strategies as well.

Sylvia Ann Hewlett conducted an extensive study of what was holding Asian professionals back in North American companies.[23] Her findings emphasized some of the same things that she had previously found for women: the importance of executive presence, which includes the idea of self-advocacy and being willing to stand out and project power through body language and voice, and a tendency to want to conform to social expectations, which worked to their disadvantage. In the case of women, there was pressure to conform to gender-role expectations that emphasized being helpful and collaborative; in the case of Asians, there was pressure to fit the stereotype of the "model minority" that succeeded through talent and hard work. Hewlett's conclusion was that for women or Asian Americans to succeed, they needed to surmount the social expectations that limited how they showed up and what they were willing to do.

Research shows that women tend to be lower than men on social dominance orientation—a preference for inequality among social groups.[24] Other data show that women are more likely to hold negative attitudes toward having power and are less likely to use reward and coercion strategies to get their own way.[25]

Some people argue that this line of argument "blames the victim" as these biases and stereotypes should not exist and people's preferences for power should not determine their career trajectories. My position, and Belmi's and Hewlett's, is that while the stereotypes and biases they represent are manifestly unfair and unjust, they exist with varying degrees of pervasiveness in many if not most organizations. Moreover, the only behavior individuals have any hope of truly controlling is their own. Therefore, the best way for people to achieve higher-level positions where they might have the leverage to change things is to recognize the rules of the game and understand what they need to do to succeed in the environment as it is presently constituted, even as they work to change that environment. And, most importantly, not to let assumptions arising from their gender, race, or social class interfere with or constrain their own definitions of who they are or what behaviors are permissible. To succeed, people need to be and feel agentic, and attempt to exercise influence and control.

In 2016, breast cancer surgeon and leader of change in medicine (and my former student) Laura Esserman was named to *Time* magazine's list of the hundred most influential people in the world. Esserman, described by some as a force of nature, comes to my class each year to help discuss the case I wrote on her. I asked her to comment on the fact that she doesn't seem to behave in gender-stereotypical ways, by swearing, getting angry, even using the "F" word. Her emailed reply:

> *I do not* choose *to be relegated to a lower status role, although many, many in power have tried. I have no problem challenging people or making them rethink their assumptions . . . I don't feel like I have to "stay in my lane" and I will not let people push me or keep me there. The dean who hired me said, "Laura, do you not see the boundaries between disciplines?" And I replied, "No, why should I?"*

You do not have to accept the limitations, or conform to the expectations, that come from your social class, gender, educational background, or race. You can enact behaviors that help you gain power—but to do so, you need to be willing to get out of your own way and to do what is required by the situations you confront.

THE CURSE OF "AUTHENTICITY"

One reason people get in their own way as they reject implementing empirically demonstrated findings on the determinants of power is their embrace of the idea of authenticity and other scientifically sketchy but uplifting leadership ideas. In their quest to be their authentic selves and display their real feelings and true opinions to others, people tell me that engaging in activities such as networking, flattering those in power, spending time ensuring that others know of their accomplishments, asking for resources, or presenting themselves to the world in a powerful fashion would not be true to who they really are. Because these behaviors often inherently entail behaving strategically in their interactions with others, building power might require people to behave inauthentically.

The idea of authentic leadership is fundamentally scientifically bogus and harmful in many ways. As two Scandinavian scholars wrote in an award-winning article that provides yet another take-down of the shoddy-to-nonexistent scholarship that undergirds the idea of authentic leaders:

> Dominant versions of positive leadership score higher on appearing good and reflecting interest in easy ideologically appealing solutions than on offering a qualified understanding of organizational life and manager-subordinate relations . . . Popular theories like transformational and authentic leadership are seriously flawed . . . The intellectual foundations they stand on are too shaky to warrant the popularity they have inspired.[26]

The critique of the idea of authenticity is not just a matter of academic rigor. As Wharton professor Adam Grant argued, "We are in the Age of Authenticity."[27] Unfortunately, as Grant continued:

Nobody wants to see your true self . . . A decade ago, the author A. J. Jacobs spent a few weeks trying to be totally authentic. He announced to an editor he would try to sleep with her if he were single and informed his nanny that he would like to go out on a date with her if his wife left him . . . He told his in-laws their conversations were boring. You can imagine how his experiment worked out. "Deceit makes our world go round," he concluded. "Without lies, marriages would crumble, workers would be fired, egos would be shattered, governments would collapse."

Authenticity is very much in keeping with the growing interest in self-disclosure. Here, too, research can shed some important insights. First, I and many social scientists acknowledge that as the line between work and personal life has blurred, opportunities to disclose personal information have multiplied. Second, there has been a "generational shift in disclosure such that younger workers view it as more appropriate and acceptable to discuss personal matters with coworkers."[28] Third, disclosing one's vulnerabilities does increase feelings of closeness: "Decades of research on self-disclosure suggest that the act of making oneself vulnerable by sharing personal information about the self typically promotes liking and feelings of closeness."[29] However, research also reveals the downsides of disclosing weaknesses, particularly in the case of task-oriented interactions for people in higher-status leadership roles. As the authors summarized, "In three laboratory experiments, we found that when higher status individuals self-disclosed a weakness, it led to lower influence . . . greater perceived conflict . . . less liking . . . and less desire for a future relationship . . . by attenuating the status of the discloser."[30]

Regardless of someone's view of authenticity, it is important to understand that the rules of power don't ask you to change your personality. Power skills and behaviors are just that—skills and behaviors that can be learned and practiced selectively as situations demand. Doing so does not necessarily dictate who you are or your personality. You can increase your strategic social interactions without becoming an extroverted networker. You can show up appearing confident even if you don't feel that way. Doing things that increase your power—that are possible to learn and implement *regardless* of who you are, if you will get out of your own way and do it—is precisely what I teach and write about.

London Business School professor Herminia Ibarra has written a *Harvard Business Review* article on what she called the authenticity paradox.[31] While Adam Grant noted that people don't necessarily want your whole, true, unvarnished self, Ibarra argued that people's quest for authenticity often leaves them stuck and unable to change when they acquire new jobs or roles requiring them to engage in different behaviors and use different skills. Her opening example was a general manager in a healthcare organization who, upon being promoted to a role that increased her number of direct reports tenfold, expressed to her people that she was nervous and unsure of herself. Ibarra reports that "her candor backfired; she lost credibility with people who wanted and needed a confident leader to take charge."[32] She commented that "learning, by definition, starts with unnatural and often superficial behaviors that can make us feel calculating instead of genuine and spontaneous."[33] But learning is essential if people are going to grow and take on greater responsibilities.

When people tell me they need to be true to themselves, I ask, which self? Their six-year-old self, their eighteen-year-old self, or another? We are changing all the time, and some—maybe a lot—of that change requires doing different things differently. After all, nobody was born walking, talking, or using the toilet. Fortunately, few of us remain authentic to our infant selves. Don't let the notion that doing something new or different—particularly if that new behavior is going to be helpful in your path to power—is inauthentic become an excuse for thinking in ways that hold you back.

Isn't Deception Eventually Uncovered?

One argument for being authentic I sometimes hear is that if you are not, your attempts at deception—for instance, flattering others or providing inaccurate information about your own motives—will be discerned, and others will hold your efforts to be anything other than your true self against you. Although a nice idea, there is precious little logic or evidence to support it.

First, people believe—and see—what they want. This simple principle underlies the study of motivated cognition, defined as "the pervasive tendency to think in ways that produce conclusions consistent with one's desires,"[34] something that occurs in multiple domains. One domain in which motivated cognition has been extensively studied is interpersonal relationships, where "biased interpretation and memory . . . assist motivated perceivers in reaching the desired conclusion that partners are responsive."[35] People are motivated to believe that others think well of them and have their interests at heart, and are conversely quite unmotivated, except in unusual circumstances, to seek to uncover deception. This is one reason why lying is so often effective. And when people perceive these others to be acting in their interest, they will have even less or no motivation to uncover any other reality.

Second, the empirical evidence on uncovering lies consistently reveals that people are largely terrible at this task. As one review noted, "People are not very accurate at detecting deception . . . In a large research literature, overall rates of lie-truth discrimination average less than 55%, when 50% would be expected by chance,"[36] with accuracy rates varying little either across studies or across people. A meta-analysis of numerous studies concluded that "people are more accurate in judging audible than visible lies, that people appear to be deceptive when motivated to be believed, and that individuals regard their interaction partners as honest."[37] That same review reported that people judge others' deceit more harshly than their own.

The combination of motivated cognition and people's generally poor ability to discern deceit means that inauthentic behavior is unlikely to be uncovered—and even if it is, sanctions are likely to be either nonexistent or minimal.

Be True to What Others Want You to Be

Phrases like "Be true to yourself" and "Find your own true north" seem excessively self-referential and are not what leaders must do to succeed. Leaders need allies and supporters; one of the primary tasks of a leader is to recruit both. This task is more readily accomplished if the leader is true not to themselves but instead to the needs and motivations of those they seek to recruit.

The story of President Lyndon Johnson, as told in Robert Caro's biographies,[38] documents a man who spent his life studying others, and in the process came to know their wants and needs. In the *American Experience* film on Johnson, historian Doris Kearns Goodwin described how the Senate, with only one hundred members, was perfect for Johnson, who could master every detail of his colleagues' personalities—their wants, needs, hopes, and fears. With that knowledge, Johnson could build relationships with them and also understand precisely how to persuade them to do what he wanted.

If you want to have allies—always a good thing if you want influence—you obviously need to provide others with something so they will support you. Maybe it is the perception of similarity— for instance, Johnson could deepen his southern accent when he talked to Southerners, and could present himself as having views consistent with those of liberal Minnesotan Hubert Humphrey and conservative Georgian Richard Russell as the occasion required. If you want others to support you, you need to be able to answer the question: What's in it for them if they do?

The biography of former California Assembly speaker and San Francisco mayor Willie Brown[39] speaks to his ability to get along with Democrats and Republicans. A Black man, he was actually put in power by conservative Republicans, yet Brown, much like Johnson, spent time raising money not for his campaigns, but for fellow Democrats, thereby endearing himself to them, too.

What is true in politics is true in organizations of all types. The people with whom you work have agendas, insecurities, problems, needs. So stop focusing on trying to figure out who you are. Instead, focus on who your *allies and potential allies* are. Become a student of the people whose support you need. The sooner you do, the faster you will develop the information and insights necessary for strategically building the alliances you need to succeed.

THE PARADOX OF "LIKABILITY"

Yet one more way people get in their own way to becoming powerful is by being overly concerned about others liking them. Social psychologist Robert Cialdini's work on influence argues that being liked is a source of power.[40] Possibly even more importantly, most people are taught from an early age to get along with others and cultivate warm interpersonal relationships. But worrying about being liked, being overly concerned with what others think about us, can get in the way of becoming powerful. A description of the late Margaret Thatcher, the long-serving British prime minister, said this: "Roy Jenkins, the cosmopolitan British statesman, observed with horrified wonder that she was 'almost totally impervious to how much she offends other people.'"[41]

Here's one problem with pursuing the goal of being liked: you may be seen as less competent. Princeton social psychologist Susan Fiske and her colleagues have extensively researched the fundamental dimensions of interpersonal perception. They have found that, across multiple cultures, the two fundamental aspects by which people judge others are warmth and competence. Her research also has uncovered that there is a tendency to see warmth and competence, although conceptually independent, as being negatively related. This relationship is nicely captured in Amy Cuddy's short but appropriately titled piece "Just Because I'm Nice, Don't Assume I'm Dumb,"[42] and in Harvard Business School faculty member Teresa Amabile's empirical study "Brilliant but Cruel." In that study, people were given actual negative and positive book reviews. "Negative reviewers were perceived as more intelligent, competent, and expert than positive reviewers, even when the content of the positive review was independently judged as being of higher quality . . . negative reviewers were perceived as significantly less likeable than positive reviewers."[43] Social psychologist Robert Cialdini's advice in a conversation with me is to first demonstrate competence. Then, if and when you show warmth, people will not see it as a sign of weakness but as something unexpected from a person with power.

There is a second problem with prioritizing likability. Particularly as people rise to higher levels in organizations, they are evaluated on their ability to get things done, not so much on how nice they are. As Gary Loveman, former CEO of Caesars Entertainment, once told my class, "If you want to be liked, get a dog. A dog will love you unconditionally." He noted that when the gaming industry fell on hard times during the 2008–2009 recession, he had to lay off thousands of people, among them single moms, cancer patients who lost their health insurance when they lost their jobs, and people who did not have much or any financial cushion. He said that he was sure that they, and their families, did not "like" him, but it was necessary to protect the organization's financial viability and the jobs of the remaining employees.

An empirical study using both longitudinal data on people's personality and careers as well as an experiment asked the provocative question "Do nice guys—and gals—really finish last?" The relevant personality dimension is agreeableness. After reviewing evidence indicating that agreeableness was negatively related to various measures of career success and also to achieving less in negotiations, this study replicated that finding using multiple rigorous methods.[44] The authors found that the negative relationship between agreeableness and salary was larger for men than for women, although it held across studies for both, partly because women were expected to be nicer than men in general, and so received a smaller penalty for being so.

In exploring what mechanisms might produce these results, the study noted that people worried about appearing agreeable might prioritize maintaining social harmony over career advancement, thereby possibly sacrificing some positive career momentum. Further, "the aspiration toward harmonious social relationships may also lead highly agreeable people to adhere excessively to social norms."[45] In the next chapter we will examine the importance of breaking the rules to rise to power. Worrying excessively about what others think of us would obviously get in the way of pursuing that strategy.

The opposite of agreeableness is, of course, disagreeableness. Berkeley business school professor Cameron Anderson and colleagues, in an innovative and well-done longitudinal study, sought to ascertain the extent to which having a disagreeable personality—being selfish, combative, and manipulative—affected people's subsequent attainment of power. They found that disagreeableness had *no* effect on subsequent power—it neither helped nor hurt. That was because disagreeableness led to two patterns of behavior that had offsetting effects on achieving power. On one hand, disagreeable people engaged in more dominant-aggressive behavior, a type of behavior that Anderson and others consistently have found *positively* predicts power. On the other, disagreeable people also engaged in fewer generous and communal behaviors, which negatively affected attaining power.[46] If disagreeableness, which their study defined in a way that clearly described someone completely unconcerned about their impact on others and willing to be reasonably nasty, had no effect on power, it seems evident that most people are too concerned much of the time about being liked.

Rukaiyah Adams, the Black woman working in the investment industry who we met in the Introduction, talked to me about letting go of the overwhelming need to be approved of and accepted that can hold people back: "I can see how wanting to achieve something meaningful that is so deeply personal, I can see how people get forceful. When you have a vision and you can see something other people can't see, I can see how you sort of have to push them into it."

Adams said two other things that I think are important to her success, both related to her surrendering the need for acceptance. She commented that she did not worry too much about "what will our board think, or will I get invited to that fancy Christmas party, or this might get me disinvited from the privileged cookout." She noted that achieving success required a combination of humility to get others on your side, and also hubris. "For women, that hubris part of it is really hard. I have to coach myself up to hubris."

Adams also talked about letting go of worrying about every relationship and what others thought. She recounted her experience with an African American man who served on a board with her.

He's from the generation of people who integrated into the larger white power structure and he's protective of that access. There are rules about Black people entering into white society, and how Black women should wear their hair and act . . . I'm just of a different era. He irritates me a lot . . . I just stopped caring if he understood. Letting go of that has made me more powerful than he is, as the board chair. That's another aspect—accepting that people just won't understand your ideas, and that's fine.

My favorite line from a rock song is from "Garden Party" by the late Ricky Nelson: "Ya can't please everyone, so ya got to please yourself." Everyone has a social identity and the obvious human need to be accepted. After all, one of the most severe punishments in military academies—or elsewhere—is social ostracism. The first rule of power is about acknowledging and accepting who you are but not letting that identity define who you will be forever. It is about understanding the importance of social connection but not letting the need for acceptance overwhelm what you want to get done, and the necessity of pursuing your own interests and agenda. It is, in short, about getting out of your own way and getting on with the task of building the power base that will provide you the leverage to accomplish your goals.

|R|U|L|E|

2

Break the Rules

SOMETIMES, WHEN YOU WANT TO ATTEND a fancy dinner where you can meet amazing people and expand your network, or create a favorable reputation owing to your ability to organize others and get things done, you have to break some rules.

Consider the actions of Christina Troitino, currently a YouTube employee and a former student in my class. Troitino described how she was able to "crash" an exclusive dinner at the Sundance Film Festival in Utah, a place where Stanford business school students mostly go to hang out with each other—something they could do in Palo Alto. Each year I challenge the students to do something at Sundance that they could not do locally, like meet some of the powerful figures that attend this major event. Troitino accepted the challenge.

To get into the fancy dinner with her boyfriend, Troitino broke one rule by showing up without announcing her "plus one." To wrangle a spot at the dinner in the first place, she defied social norms and conventional expectations by cadging an invitation to a prestigious, closed event instead of passively waiting years to achieve the status that would have made such an invitation automatic. Troitino described how she did this:

> I noticed this very private, very exclusive dinner series that's [been] going on for 10 plus years called [name withheld]. This year [2020], I noticed they were doing their own mini-conference within the festival to push a nonprofit they were trying to start. I thought, this is the year I want to get into one of these dinners. I found some generic email, hello@[name].com, and I wrote them a one-sentence message: "Hey, I'm Christina. I write for Forbes. Can I attend one of the dinners?" I figured out they had two really awesome dinners, one was with Alice Waters [founder of Chez Panisse and a legend in food] and one with Martha Stewart. I figured I could see Waters as she was in the Bay Area. I got an email back from someone who worked on the PR team for them and they said, "We have the Alice Waters dinner on Friday and a Martha Stewart dinner on Saturday. Are any of these of interest to you?" I consciously waited 48 hours to respond to signal, "Wow, this person must be so important that a dinner even with Martha Stewart is a lower priority on their to-do list." I eventually responded that I was busy on Friday [which she was not] but I could probably do the Saturday one. On Saturday morning I wake up and they had sent me an RSVP link. The form asks if I want to bring a plus one or not. I didn't know what Ben wanted to do. So I just show up with Ben. The guest list person asked for my name. I tell them. Then they ask who I'm with. I say with Ben. "Oh, we didn't have you down for a plus one." The two staff members look at each other and say, "Fine, we'll have both of you come in." I definitely had to use a lot of path to power techniques to just muscle my way in, breaking some rules and making myself seem a lot more important than I actually am.

Troitino was not finished with her initiatives. When the COVID-19 pandemic began, she launched what was called Team Positivity Contagion to figure out how to do virtual social events to keep students connected while everyone was socially distant. The Stanford group made a guidebook that they shared with other schools so "they could turn on a similar platform overnight." Eventually Stanford, in the person of Troitino, decided to do a charity fundraiser event to bring all the schools together, which came to be called the MBA Battle Royale. Troitino continued:

> *Someone half-jokingly said it would be great if we get this guy MBA Mikey, who has a famous Instagram account that posts funny memes specific to the MBA experience, who has hundreds of thousands of followers. I just sent him a three-sentence message, "Hey, I go to Stanford. We're trying to put together a cross-MBA program virtual charity event. Do you want in?" And he replied within an hour, "Yes, I'm in." And soon these influencers were promoting the event, making it seem way more legitimate than we had intended. The 10th school to reach out to us was Harvard, which they did because there was such a critical mass of other programs involved. When people ask me, "Who in Stanford approved this?" I said, "No one." Stanford loved this because it made them look good because of the good press. In the end we raised $56,000. From start to finish, putting the event together and running it was about a month. And now all the schools involved have already asked to do it proactively again next year. Because I was the one reaching out to all these other schools, I got a lot of credit. And people reached out with questions about random, non-related things. They knew we were in the leadership position.*

Breaking the rules in this second example meant fundamentally taking the initiative—not waiting to obtain permission or, for that matter, even asking for anyone's approval, but just creating things—in this case, an event. By so doing, Troitino put herself in a central network position and built a brand as someone who gets stuff done.

Troitino obviously enjoyed some advantages besides her willingness to break the rules—she was a graduate student at a prestigious university. But her example illustrates what I believe to be general principles about rule breaking that apply to virtually anyone in any situation.

WHY AND HOW RULE BREAKING WORKS TO CREATE POWER

Rule breaking and violating social norms to build power fundamentally entail undertaking behaviors—taking initiatives—that are "different" and unexpected. Most importantly, rule breaking requires being proactive and *doing* something—in Christina's case, initiating contact with sponsors of a prestigious dinner and starting a cross-business school activity.

Several psychological mechanisms support the idea that violating norms, rules, and social conventions can make rule breakers seem more powerful and thereby create power for them. Here are some explanations for why and how.

The Heuristic Association Between Power and Norm Violation

A study in *Social Psychological and Personality Science* concluded, "When people have power, they act the part. Powerful people smile less, interrupt others, and speak in a louder voice . . . The powerful have fewer rules to follow."[1] Or, phrased another way by Lord Acton and empirically demonstrated by social psychologist David Kipnis,[2] power corrupts and absolute power corrupts absolutely. This heuristic association between power and rule breaking—the powerful are freer to defy social norms and conventions and get away with it, and thus, powerful people are more likely to enact socially inappropriate behavior—prompted University of Amsterdam–based social scientist Gerben van Kleef and colleagues to ask if breaking rules could actually cause the rule breakers to seem more powerful. In a series of experimental studies using multiple methods, including a scenario, a film clip, and face-to-face interaction, the answer was "yes."[3]

In their first study, participants were told to imagine they were in a crowded waiting room in city hall seeking to renew their passport. In the norm-violating condition, someone got up and took a cup of coffee from the coffee can when the service desk was empty. In the control condition, the person got up, went to the restroom, and returned, so in both cases the individual engaged in some action. In the norm-violation condition, the individual who took the coffee was rated as 21 percent more powerful than the person who just went to the restroom.

The second study provided a scenario in which a bookkeeper was told about an anomaly in a financial report. In the norm-violation condition, the bookkeeper said that things like this happen all the time, it was unlikely that the external accountants would notice, and occasionally you can bend the rules a little, if necessary. In the control condition, the bookkeeper said that they needed to take the incident seriously, and although the external accountants were unlikely to catch it, they needed to follow the rules. The bookkeeper who broke the rules was rated higher on power and also on volitional capacity, or the freedom to do whatever they wanted.

In the third study, people watched a video of an open-air cafeteria. In the norm-violation condition, an actor put his feet on another chair, lit a cigarette, and repeatedly dropped ashes on the floor. He also spoke more rudely to a waiter. In this study, the norm violator was perceived to be 29 percent more powerful than the actor in the control condition, who was more polite to the waiter, flicked their ashes in an ashtray, and crossed their legs instead of putting his feet on another chair.

The fourth study involved direct interaction with the norm violator rather than a video or a scenario. When people arrived for the study, a confederate of the experimenter behaved inappropriately in numerous ways throughout the interaction. They arrived late, threw their bag on the table in front of the couches on which the participant was sitting, and put their feet on the table, among other things. Once again, the norm violator was perceived as more powerful. All of the differences in these studies were statistically significant.

In the opening of the article reporting the experiments, van Kleef and his coauthors wrote, "One would hope, perhaps, that powerholders who break the rules fall from grace and lose their power . . . Or might the very act of breaking the rules actually fuel perceptions of power?"[4] Norm violators who are not sanctioned gain power from their ability to violate the rules, signaling they are different from and more powerful than people who (presumably must) adhere to social expectations. This passage helps to explain why Donald Trump's lying has not caused him more difficulties. Lying, which violates the social norm to tell the truth, is frequently not sanctioned, and because it also violates expectations, actually increases perceptions of the person's power. There are obviously limits to the positive effect of norm violations on perceptions of power, but the idea that violating rules and social conventions might increase someone's power is a principle that ought to be taken seriously. The idea helps explain many aspects of social life in workplaces, not just in politics.

Note that Christina Troitino engaged in a series of small but important behaviors that would be unexpected from someone in a low-power position. She sent a very short email asking about the dinners without providing an extensive personal biography, only describing herself as a writer for *Forbes*. She waited forty-eight hours to respond to the email explaining her dinner options. And she showed up with an uninvited guest without letting the organizers know in advance. In this way, she acted as if she had the power to break with expectations and do what she wanted. Possibly because of these behaviors, she was able to get herself (and her partner) into a highly exclusive dinner.

Rule Breaking Surprises Others

Because most people follow the rules most of the time, people who don't can and often do catch their interaction partners off guard. This element of surprise can work to the perpetrator's advantage, because others do not have time to prepare for the interaction and decide how they want to respond.

Consider the case of Jason Calacanis, an internet entrepreneur, angel (early-stage) investor, author, and podcaster. When Jason was college age, his middle-class family suffered some serious financial reversals. Calacanis wanted to go to Fordham. The head of admissions there at the time was Ed Boland. While Calacanis was attending Brooklyn College, he took a tae kwon do class at Fordham, and he used this as an excuse to "drop in" unannounced on the head of admissions. He told me:

> Before I would go, I would find somebody to write me a letter of recommendation. I'd knock on Mr. Boland's door and I'd hand it to him. And he'd say "Jason, do we have an appointment? Are you on my schedule?" And I'd say, "No, I'm here for the tae kwon do class. I wanted to give you this letter of recommendation. And I thought you should see my second quarter grades" . . . Mr. Boland calls and says, "I'm going to Yale . . . But as I was leaving, they asked me if I had any requests as to how they could do things better. And I said I thought they should accept the most nontraditional student for the 1988 year . . . You."[5]

Still, Calacanis needed financial help to continue at Fordham. He was often behind on tuition payments, and he was not permitted to register for his junior year. He described what he did:

Okay, what works? Going to the top works . . . Everybody in between doesn't matter. So I walked into the dean's office and asked if the dean was in. And the woman at the desk said, "He's in his office." I said "Thanks" and walked in. I said, "Dean, I'm Jason Calacanis. I've really enjoyed my years here but I am going to have to drop out." And he said, "Do you have an appointment?" I told him no but that I really needed to talk to him.[6]

To make a long story short, at the end of the interaction, Calacanis had a job at the computer lab in the business school earning $8 an hour compared to the $3.50 he had been making at another job. Calacanis noted that these interactions emboldened him to take chances.

Calacanis walked into people's offices without an appointment, thereby breaking the rules of how you interact with powerful people—or maybe expectations of how you should approach anyone. Caught off guard and surprised by his audacity, the admissions director was impressed enough with Calacanis's drive to get him admitted to Fordham. And the dean, surprised and lacking a plan for how to handle Calacanis's financial situation, reacted on the spot by connecting him with the business school computer lab, where he then more than doubled his wages.

Surprise works not only because it catches people off guard but also because it affects people's cognitions and emotions. Tania Luna, a former psychology instructor at Hunter College and currently co-CEO of LifeLabs Learning, has written a book about the neurobiology of surprises. In a radio interview with PRI, Luna noted that surprises cause "humans to physically freeze for 1/25th of a second. Then they usually trigger something in the brain . . . a moment that causes humans to generate extreme curiosity in an attempt to figure out what is happening . . . Surprises also intensify emotions."[7] Surprises cause people to pay more attention to satisfy their curiosity—and if you want to be remembered, having people pay closer attention to their interactions with you is probably a good thing.

It Is Easier—and More Effective—to Ask Forgiveness Than Permission

Although conflict is common in workplaces, with one study showing that employees spent on average almost three hours each week
engaged in conflict, some 60 percent of workers never receive any
basic training in dealing with conflict situations.[8] This absence of
training, coupled with people's desire to be liked and accepted,
means that most difficult situations are avoided rather than being
confronted, and most people are conflict averse and therefore seek
to avoid arguments.

In practical terms for exercising power, this means that resistance to what you want to do is likely to be less than you expect
because people will be reluctant to confront you and risk a difficult
interpersonal conversation. Therefore, it is easier and often more
successful and productive to just do what you want and to ask
forgiveness for something that you have done instead of seeking
permission for it beforehand. Once you have completed or accomplished something, it becomes a fait accompli and difficult to undo.
Moreover, the benefits and consequences of what you have done are
no longer hypothetical but real, which also makes others reluctant
to undo what you have done and thereby destroy the benefits produced. Once Troitino had created a successful cross-school event,
who was going to criticize her for raising money for charity while
providing a fun experience to numerous students—even though
she had asked no one's permission to organize the event?

Robert Moses, New York's master builder, who wielded immense
power over a forty-year career, was a genius in employing the strategy of turning his plans into physical reality—even before he had
permission to do so. Often Moses would start his projects prior to
obtaining all of the necessary permits and sometimes even the fund-
ing to complete them. He understood that once a park or playground
was constructed, it was much more difficult and less likely for others
to undo his creations. His first foray in park development was to turn

the Taylor Estate in East Islip, Long Island, into a park, now called Hecksher State Park. There is little doubt that Moses overstepped his legal authority in seizing private property and using unappropriated monies to begin developing it. As described by Robert Caro in his Pulitzer Prize–winning biography of Moses:

> *Moses had never stopped developing the Taylor Estate . . . By the time the higher courts came to rule on the question of whether the Taylor Estate was a park, it* was *a park. What was a judge to do? Tell the state to tear up the roads and tear down the buildings . . . Tell the people who had visited the Taylor Estate that they could visit it no more?[9]*

Caro commented on the lesson Moses had learned: "Once you did something physically, it was very hard for even a judge to undo it."[10] In fact, once anything is done, it is harder to undo—and that includes instituting awards, events, and ceremonies. Do something first, and sort out the consequences later—even if this breaks some rules.

Rules Tend to Favor the Already Strong

Another advantage to breaking with the rules is that, not surprisingly, rules and norms tend to favor those with the power to make them—who tend to be the entities in power. Why play by rules others have made that may disadvantage you?

A stunning illustration of this principle is the study by political scientist Ivan Arreguín-Toft titled *How the Weak Win Wars*.[11] He studied actual wars in which the difference in power—armaments, size of armies, and so forth—between the strong and weak was at least five times. Between 1800 and 2003, the stronger force won 71.5 percent of the time. Arreguín-Toft noted something interesting when he broke his analyses down by time period: between 1950 and 1999, the weak actually won more often than the strong, 51.2 percent of the time. His book explores why, and the insights are the foundation for Malcolm Gladwell's deservedly acclaimed *New*

Yorker article "How David Beats Goliath."[12] When underdogs don't play by the conventional rules—when they employ an unconventional strategy—their winning percentage increases from 28.5 to 63.6 percent.

What is true in war is also true in basketball—teams that use a full-court press 100 percent of the time they are on defense outperform their natural talents and win disproportionately frequently. People who make their own rules—who do the unexpected—often succeed in ways they could not have anticipated.

And what is true in war and basketball is also true in business. Many successful entrepreneurs, particularly those seeking to disrupt existing industries and business models, are notorious rule breakers. An extreme if well-known example: Elon Musk, the CEO of electric car and battery manufacturer Tesla. Musk has succeeded by violating the conventional wisdom that it is important to get along with regulators. Instead, he has taken them on and often insulted them. An article in the *Wall Street Journal* noted:

> *Elon Musk has emerged as a winner in a series of run-ins with a range of regulatory agencies that have watched as he sidestepped rules or ignored enforcement attempts . . . not letting regulations hinder his goals to revolutionize transportation with Tesla Inc.'s electric cars or colonize Mars using SpaceX rockets . . . Rather than engaging in a give-and-take with government authorities, Mr. Musk's default response includes making public, sometimes crude, remarks via Twitter disparaging them.[13]*

Here's the difficulty in the advice to disregard rules and social expectations. As I explore in the next section of this chapter, playing by the rules, following conventional wisdom, is a potent behavior-directing force. People like to play by the rules, regardless of the results. According to Gladwell, once George Washington began achieving victories over the British Army during the US war of independence, he had his men dress up and march in formation just like the British, until sad experience forced him to resume hiding behind trees and rock formations and plotting ambushes. Basketball teams that won using the full-court press all the time often returned to playing a more conventional defense, notwithstanding their greater success pursuing a less conventional strategy. Asymmetric warfare and unconventional strategies may bring success and power, but to break the rules, people need to be able to stand the resulting social disapproval.

THE DILEMMA: TO FIT IN OR STAND OUT

Most people, most of the time, *don't* break the rules, and for very good reason. The world is filled with rules that others expect you to follow. Everyone in a role such as parent, employee, doctor, teacher—which is everyone, since we all fill multiple roles—confronts social expectations about what you are to do and how you are to behave in that role. To illustrate the enormous psychological power of such expectations, my colleague, the late Jerry Salancik, on the first day of class at the University of Illinois, came in and sat among the students. He did not say anything. It was obvious because of his age and attire that he was the instructor. But he temporarily violated the expectations about how teachers are supposed to behave, including where they were supposed to position themselves. He told me how uncomfortable the students became, even hostile, the longer he refused to behave consistently with the role expectations for his position. Salancik taught his students the potency of role expectations, and his example teaches us how uncomfortable it is to break the rules.

The world is filled with social conventions, behaviors like saying "please" and "thank you," modulating your voice, dressing in appropriate ways. There are also many pieces of conventional wisdom—lessons about how to climb the corporate ladder, how to be a leader, and how to be a good subordinate—and they are treated as rules.

People are expected to know the rules and adhere to them, partly because these rules help social interaction proceed smoothly. From infancy, people are taught, first by their parents, then by institutions such as schools and religious organizations, and later by their employers, what they are supposed to do. They can be expelled from school, excommunicated by their religion, and fired from their employer for violating the rules. Even more painfully, on occasion they can be socially ostracized.

If you follow the rules, you will fit in, and fitting in is important to people. We are, of course, social creatures who crave the companionship and company of others. Social psychology and sociology, among other disciplines, provide evidence that the pressure to conform to what others think, and to adhere to what others expect us to do, is enormous.

The dilemma is that while people want to fit in and be accepted and not ostracized for violating social norms, people also want to stand out. If people blend in too perfectly, they become unnoticeable, undifferentiated from those around them competing for promotions. People also want to excel, and to excel is to be, almost by definition, different. As the two examples that began this chapter well illustrate, standing out, breaking the rules, often is a path to success. The famous author and magazine editor Tina Brown told *60 Minutes* about getting thrown out of boarding schools (notice the plural). Steve Jobs and Bill Gates both dropped out of college, defying what suburban, middle-class children were supposed to do.

Because of how people are socialized and the desire to be accepted by others—which we believe comes from adhering to rules for behavior—most people, most of the time, follow conventional wisdom and willingly follow rules that *others*—and this is the important point, often *others* with more power and interests quite different from their own—have promulgated. The lesson of this chapter is that, notwithstanding these numerous forces pushing rule following and conformity, many paths to power entail parting with expectations, disregarding conventional wisdom, and breaking rules—except the rule of this chapter, which is to break the rules.

BREAK THE RULES BY ASKING FOR THINGS

One behavioral norm that is particularly strong in Western societies is the belief in self-sufficiency and the corresponding notion that it is intrusive and inappropriate to ask others for assistance. My Stanford colleague Frank Flynn and his coauthor Vanessa Lake conducted a series of studies that demonstrated that people were reluctant to ask for help and that they vastly overestimated the number of people they would need to approach to get others to do them a favor. Flynn and Lake wrote that "help seeking has been described as an uncomfortable, if not embarrassing act that requires a modicum of courage . . . In addition to appearing inadequate or incompetent, most people fear the possibility of rejection."[14]

Their studies showed, across a variety of settings, that people often overestimated by a factor of two the number of people they would need to approach to get, for instance, three people to let them borrow their cell phone for a short call, to fill out a short questionnaire, or to walk with them to the Columbia University gym. Flynn and Lake hypothesized and found that the reason for this overestimation is that requestors were overly focused on the cost of complying with the request and could not sufficiently put themselves in the place of the person receiving the request. Complying with requests is almost automatic as people like to see themselves as cooperative and benevolent and, in many instances, the costs of the favor being requested were trivial.

The Flynn and Lake studies revealed something else important: people tended to drop out of the studies at an inordinately high rate, because they experienced the relatively trivial experimental task of asking strangers for a favor as particularly aversive. For instance, in the study asking people to ask others to borrow a cell phone or walk them to the gym, 27 percent of the people who initially agreed to be in the study dropped out once they found out what they had to do. After asking fifty-two students who agreed to participate in the study to ask people to fill out a short questionnaire, six people dropped out immediately and three others failed to complete the task. These data are completely consistent with the idea that, as Flynn and Lake noted, "help seeking is uncomfortable."

But people want to offer help. First of all, it is consistent with social expectations to be cooperative. Also, asking for help is flattering. In asking for the advice or assistance of another, the requestor implicitly elevates the status of the target, who is in the position of bestowing a favor, earning gratitude, and most importantly, demonstrating their importance to the requestor by complying with the request. Consequently, in the spirit of rule breaking, and consistent with the Flynn and Lake results, people should ask for more.

When Keith Ferrazzi, marketing guru and best-selling author, graduated from Harvard Business School in 1992, he was deciding between accepting a job at the consulting firms McKinsey or Deloitte Consulting:

> "We tried to talk Keith into coming to join us over McKinsey," recalled Pat Loconto, the former head of Deloitte. "Before he accepted, however, he insisted on seeing the 'head guys' as he would call them." Loconto agreed to meet Ferrazzi at an Italian restaurant in New York City. "After we had a few drinks . . . Keith said he would accept the offer on one condition—he and I would have dinner once a year at the same restaurant . . . So I promised to have dinner with him once a year and that's how we recruited him . . . That way, he was guaranteed access to the top."[15]

A bold move, for sure. But what is the downside? Often the worst thing that can happen if you ask for something, like a dinner with the CEO, is rejection, being told no. But people probably weren't going to get what they had asked for in the absence of asking for it in any event, so nothing is really lost. Maybe people suffer the sting of being turned down. Most good salespeople will tell you that if you can't stand being rejected, don't go into sales—and everyone is selling themselves and their ideas all the time. Get used to asking, being turned down, and asking again, or for different things from different people. Asking does break some rules, but it works. Flynn and Lake's article title says it all: "If you need help, just ask."

Like every rule outlined in this book, there is no reason to believe what I describe does not work for almost anyone, regardless of race or gender. Consider the case of Reginald Lewis, the first African American to run a $1 billion enterprise (TLC Beatrice International Holdings), a graduate of Harvard Law School, and a very successful private equity investor. Lewis, who grew up in Baltimore, graduated from Virginia State University with a degree in political science in 1965. That summer, the Rockefeller Foundation sponsored a program at Harvard to try and introduce African Americans to the study of law and get the participants well equipped to get into law school. The program had two "rules." First, the applicants should be juniors, so they could take the learnings back and use them during their senior year as they applied to law school. Second, the one law school that they should not think of applying to was Harvard—the program was designed to help them become interested in and get into other places.

Lewis, notwithstanding the fact that he had already graduated, wrangled admission to the summer program. During that summer, he did his best to stand out and perform at a high level. And then he met with a law-faculty-member advisor to the program and pitched the idea that Harvard Law School would benefit from having Reginald Lewis as part of its student body. As nicely described in the "No Application Required" chapter of his autobiography, *Why Should White Guys Have All the Fun?*,[16] against all odds Lewis was admitted to Harvard Law, in contravention of the "rule" that precluded precisely that. Following their decision to admit him, the school had him complete the formalities by filling out an application. This made Lewis "the only person in the 148-year history of

Harvard to be accepted before even applying."[17] Lewis noted that asking for admission to the school while in the summer program was risky, and he prepared well for the lunchtime conversation, mustering and rehearsing his arguments in advance and dressing up. But as he noted, and consistent with the theme of this chapter, what did he have to lose? He wasn't going to Harvard Law in the fall, so he might as well take a chance, make his case, and the worst that could happen is that he wouldn't go to Harvard that fall. Lewis's life as a lawyer and private equity investor was filled with instances of his not adhering to rules or conforming to expectations. That willingness to take chances, coupled with Lewis's manifest talents and abilities, is precisely what made him successful.

RULE BREAKING AND CHANGE

Rules and social conventions are made by those in power, mostly to ensure that their power is perpetuated. Therefore, some of the rules, some of the social norms and expectations, may be sensible, but many are probably not—at best they are arbitrary, at worst seriously harmful to those with less power.

When Rosa Parks, a Black woman, refused to sit in the back of the bus, she violated a social norm designed to keep African Americans in a subordinate status. When Martin Luther King Jr. wrote his famous "Letter from a Birmingham Jail," he was indeed in jail. The history of the US civil rights movement is one of people refusing to accept norms and actual laws that kept people of color from enjoying the same rights, including the right to vote, enjoyed by others. The late congressman and civil rights activist John Lewis at the end of his life admonished people to get into trouble, what he called "good trouble," to challenge laws and taken-for-granted practices that disenfranchised and demeaned people of color. Nelson Mandela served twenty-seven years in a South African prison because he dared to break rules and violate the social expectations at the foundation for apartheid.

Although these examples are dramatic and vivid, they illustrate the general principle that rules are made by people in power mostly to perpetuate that power. Therefore, if existing power arrangements are going to change, people are going to have to break those rules and violate social norms to create a different social order.

Similar processes occur in work organizations. The gender-role expectation that women should not display anger or evince too much open ambition, and be more communal in their approach to issues, all disadvantage women in the contest for career advancement, where they compete against men who more comfortably display power through anger and fulfill their ambitions—often with at least tacit permission.

Social expectations for how women and people of color are supposed to behave, both subtle and overt, disadvantage those who conform to those expectations. This phenomenon is sometimes called the "double bind" because violating norms often provokes backlash and resentment on the part of those benefiting from those norms.

Without for a moment denying the dilemma that unfair and unjust rules pose, I think organizational participants can take an important lesson from the social movements that have sought racial and economic justice. Yes, Martin Luther King—the very individual for whom there is a national holiday—was under FBI surveillance and was, toward the end of his life, not always lauded by those who saw his demands as a threat. He was, in fact, despised in some circles because of his pushing for economic justice and his opposition to the Vietnam War. But recall the lesson from the last chapter about not worrying excessively about being liked. If you are going to "change lives, change organizations, and change the world," to slightly paraphrase my employer's motto, you should expect to encounter resistance and pushback, sometimes quite intense. Change invariably requires the reallocation of resources, and those from whom resources are moving are not going to be happy about that prospect. Changes in career trajectories that provide opportunities to previously underrepresented groups mean more competition and possibly fewer opportunities for others who previously enjoyed less competition.

In short, I see the double-bind dilemma but do not really think, in the end, people have any choice. To follow rules and adhere to social expectations that disadvantage you in your path to power is to consign yourself to unduly limited opportunities and prospects. Thus, for those who seek power, particularly those seeking it from positions of disadvantage, breaking the rules is the only possible, sensible option. Simply put, if you are going to win given the rules in place, by all means follow and advocate for those rules. For everyone else less guaranteed of inevitable success, rule breaking, the second rule of power, provides an empirically validated—and virtually the only feasible—path to success.

|R|U|L|E|
3

Appear Powerful

In April 2010, Lloyd Blankfein, then the CEO of Goldman Sachs, the prominent investment bank and financial services company, appeared before a US Senate committee. Goldman stood accused of short-selling (betting against) securities it had sold its clients, an action that struck some people as a conflict of interest and a breach of trust. On June 17 of that year, Tony Hayward, then the CEO of multinational oil company BP, appeared before a US House of Representatives committee. The committee was investigating the explosion on a BP drilling platform in the Gulf of Mexico that had killed eleven employees and caused an enormous, ongoing release of oil with substantial ecological damage. The subsequent career trajectories of the two CEOs could not have been more different.

On July 17, 2010, BP announced that Hayward would be replaced by Bob Dudley as CEO on October 1. Meanwhile, Blankfein continued to serve as CEO of Goldman until the end of 2018, when he stepped out of the role on his own terms and at a time of his choosing.

Although there are obviously numerous differences between the two situations, what is strikingly obvious if one watches the two leaders testify is the difference in their demeanor, language, and approach—differences that undoubtedly extended beyond these specific appearances. Hayward is mostly apologetic and restrained, both verbally and physically, as he sits hunched over and uses few hand or arm movements. Blankfein is more confrontational and forceful in his self-presentation.

I use edited clips from their testimony, both with and (to focus the class on body language) without sound, to make what I consider one of the most obvious but important points in understanding power. How you "show up" is important, maybe even determinative, of your career trajectory, how much power and status others accord you, and whether you keep your job. Regardless of your formal title, there is inevitably some degree of uncertainty or ambiguity about your potency and strength. Therefore, others will assess you to ascertain how seriously to take you, whether to defer to you and perhaps ally with you. As the late social psychologist Nalini Ambady noted, "The ability to form impressions of others is a critical human skill."[1]

Research shows that people form impressions of others, often precise assessments of personality, very quickly, using "thin slices"—just a few seconds—of behavior. People then make subsequent decisions and judgments about others using those small snippets of behavior. Research also demonstrates that even these quickly formed first impressions are surprisingly durable. Their persistence arises in part because of the pervasiveness of confirmation bias, the tendency to seek and interpret evidence in ways consistent with existing beliefs or expectations.[2] Therefore, if you want to attain and maintain power, the third rule of power is to appear powerful, because others will treat you and make decisions about you depending on how you show up, and those decisions will often act in ways to make the initial impressions become true. For instance, if people think you are not too smart or competent, they will ask you questions that preclude your demonstrating how much you know, and give you few opportunities to demonstrate your intelligence and competence. As the social psychologist Robert Cialdini once insightfully remarked to me, you only get one chance to make a first impression.

Let us compare the two CEOs' testimony. Hayward reads a prepared opening statement, taking about six minutes. As the average person speaks approximately 130 to 150 words per minute,[3] that opening statement is only about 900 words—he could have recited it from memory. Reading precludes his making frequent, continuous eye contact with his audience. Research going back decades has demonstrated that (1) eye contact increases speakers' credibility and the perception of their honesty;[4] (2) the duration of eye contact affects observers' judgments of someone's potency, including their leadership;[5] and (3) eye contact affects people's perceptions of the speaker's self-esteem and causes others to rate the speaker more favorably.[6] Moreover, Hayward reading that opening statement makes him appear scripted and insincere—maybe those words are not his own, provided by lawyers or staff.

Showing up without notes, appearing to be in command of the subject matter and the situation, is important. The late Jack Valenti, head of the Motion Picture Association of American for some thirty-eight years, told me that when he appeared on Capitol Hill, he never came with written notes, because he wanted to seem as if he was in command of the facts and, without needing to look at written materials, could engage more directly with the audience. The first recommendation about showing up in a powerful way: don't use notes or a lot of other props or cues, particularly things that would cause you not to make eye contact with the person or people you are speaking with.

Hayward is apologetic, and also, in response to a question, argues that as CEO of a company that drills hundreds of wells each year all over the world, he had no involvement in the drilling of this particular well, "none whatsoever." Most importantly, he never places BP and its actions in context. How old is the company? How many people does it employ in the US? What are its activities and how do those activities affect economic activity and employment, for instance, in the Gulf Coast region? Why is BP drilling in the Gulf of Mexico under difficult conditions in the first place? Hayward promises an investigation into the causes of the disaster and compensation to remediate the economic damage caused by the spill, but does little to convey that the situation is under control and that a similar accident will not happen again. Most importantly, Hayward does little to defend the work, honor, or prestige of BP and its employees. He is, as one former student who was and is a senior executive at BP wrote me, neither forceful nor particularly remorseful.

Blankfein, by contrast, seems completely at ease, smiling often when he is not reacting quizzically to the questions being asked, as if to communicate that the questioners don't understand the issues. He explains—many times—the role of Goldman as a financial intermediary and market maker. He talks about the age of the firm and its leading role in the financial services industry, including its prestige and size, the fact that the clients' trust is essential, and the expertise of its highly skilled workforce. He insists that Goldman was only doing what its (knowledgeable and sophisticated) clients wanted: standing on the other side of transactions they sought to execute and providing them the risks, for instance in the housing market, that they sought. His demeanor signals that he is comfortable with what Goldman has done, as he repeatedly explains how financial markets work and Goldman's various roles in those markets. In three hours of testimony (Hayward was before his committee for some nine hours), Blankfein never *once* apologizes for Goldman's actions or backs away from his argument about what market makers do and their right—indeed, responsibility—to engage in hedging activities, including shorting securities they have sold.

The consequences of how you show up for your power and your career is true not just if you are the CEO of a company facing serious challenges, but also if you are someone applying for a job or seeking a promotion. As I make clear in this chapter, language—and body language—matters for how others judge us, and those judgments have consequences. It is not by accident that Amy Cuddy's TED talk on body language[7] is one of the most watched, and that her book, *Presence*,[8] was a best-seller. Here's why appearing powerful is so important, and some more advice about how to do so.

APPEARANCE MATTERS AND PREDICTS

Consider the following study. Thirteen college teachers of a variety of subjects are videotaped, and short (three ten-second) *silent* segments from different portions of their classes are shown to nine undergraduates, who are instructed to rate the teachers on several dimensions such as confidence, dominance, honesty, and empathy. The research question: Do the average ratings (across the nine raters) of very short, silent clips of teacher appearance and behavior correlate with the course evaluations—ratings—provided by the actual students who took full classes from these thirteen individuals and therefore observed them over many weeks? The possibly surprising answer: not only are the ratings of the short, silent clips correlated significantly with real student evaluations, the correlations are quite high. For instance, the raters' ratings of confidence is correlated .82 with instructor ratings, dominance is correlated .79, being enthusiastic .76, and being optimistic .84 with actual student course ratings.[9]

The study's authors interpret these data as showing that thin slices of nonverbal behavior reliably reflect actual qualities of the individual. Here is another interpretation of the study results—and one that is consistent with the point of this chapter. Both the students in their evaluations of teaching effectiveness and the raters of how people seem based on the short, silent videos are responding similarly to nonverbal cues about energy, potency, confidence, and other individual characteristics that, although somewhat irrelevant to whether someone can actually convey material effectively to students, are quite relevant to how those individuals are judged. Both the raters—and the students—are responding to how people *appear*.

And not only does appearance matter in the classroom. Nalini Ambady, one of the coauthors of the course evaluation study, coauthored another study that asked the question "Are impressions of chief executive officers . . . related to the performance of their companies?"[10] In a study of fifty *Fortune* 500 companies, one hundred undergraduates rated the pictures of the CEOs either for overall leadership ability or for five traits—competence, dominance, likability, maturity, and trustworthiness. The study found that "ratings of power-related traits from CEO's faces," even after statistically controlling for age, affect, and attractiveness, were significantly related to company profits, as were the ratings of CEO leadership.[11] Although this first study had only male CEOs as targets for ratings, a subsequent study replicated the results with companies led by women.[12] The results beg the question as to "whether more successful companies choose individuals with a particular appearance to be their CEOs or whether individuals with a particular appearance emerge as more successful in their work as CEOs."[13] Notwithstanding which interpretation is correct—and both may be true—the connection between appearance and leader success has been uncovered in numerous domains besides business and is a reliable, replicated finding.

These empirical results are why it is fair and accurate to say that in numerous ways, and in many different contexts and settings, appearance matters and predicts career outcomes and attributions of power. Without boring you to death with the extensive research literature on this topic, here are a few more relevant highlights:

- A study, proceeding from the premise that "implicit trait inferences from facial appearance can bias everyday life," found that people whose faces were judged to be more trustworthy and distressed-looking received higher priority from triage nurses in emergency rooms.[14]

- A study using data on hundreds of thousands of Swedish males examined the oft-observed relationship between height and earnings in which tall people earn more. The authors found evidence that the relationship between height and earnings reflected family background and also the association between height and cognitive and noncognitive skills.[15]

- In addition to height, physical attractiveness has been consistently found to predict higher earnings[16] and other positive career outcomes such as greater likelihood of employment[17] and recommendations for promotion.[18] A recent meta-analysis of sixty-nine studies concluded that, compared to people with average attractiveness, highly attractive individuals earn 20 percent more and are recommended for promotion more frequently.[19] One reason for this relationship: attractive individuals possess a small advantage in human capital and a larger advantage in social capital, in part because of their increased visibility and the greater willingness of others to provide mentorship and advice.

Nonrational, Automatic Responses to Appearing Powerful

People's reactions to the physical and behavioral appearance of power is at least partly instinctual and subconscious. Our forebears, in order to survive, had to be able to quickly ascertain friend from foe and also who was likely to prevail in the struggle for dominance. Therefore, the ability to quickly size others up was—and is—an evolutionarily adaptive skill. Consequently, "We form first impressions from faces despite warnings not do so. Moreover, there is considerable agreement in our impressions, which carry significant social outcomes. Appearance matters because some facial qualities are so useful in guiding adaptive behavior that even a trace of those qualities can create an impression."[20] Of course, these automatic responses are not invariably accurate. However, "the errors produced by these overgeneralizations are presumed to be less maladaptive than those that might result from failing to respond appropriately to persons who vary in fitness, age, emotion, or familiarity."[21]

Although we like to think of ourselves as rational beings, many of our decisions are guided by emotion—affect. Marketing professor Baba Shiv has extensively studied the role of emotions in choice.[22] Fundamentally, when time and attention—cognitive resources—are limited, decisions are influenced more by affect than by thought. This situation is typical of daily living, in which we seldom cogitate about decisions but react quickly, mindlessly, and emotionally to situations as they come at us in rapid succession. The implication: the influence of physical appearance and body language on our responses to others is mostly going to occur outside of conscious awareness—one reason it is hard to overcome.

UNDERSTAND WHO YOUR AUDIENCE REALLY IS—AND WHAT THEY WANT AND NEED FROM YOU

At this point you are probably thinking, this research on how important appearance is may be interesting, but unless one is going to undergo various cosmetic surgery procedures, what is the relevance? Although people cannot radically change their physiognomy, they *can* do things to increase their physical attractiveness and the appearance of height, in part by paying attention to grooming, colors, and wardrobe choices that play to one's strengths and accentuate the positive aspects of appearance. Best of all, as the examples that began this chapter illustrate, people can—and should—do things with facial expressions, body language, the words they use, and all the other aspects that go into "appearing powerful" to project as much power and influence as they can. Berkeley social psychologist Dana Carney, an expert on nonverbal behavior, has noted, "Conveying power through nonverbal behavior is easy to do—whether or not you actually have it . . . the behaviors to express [power] are easy to select and deploy."[23] As this chapter makes clear, people can do a great deal to both project power and avoid seeming small and diminished.

Most fundamentally, people can ascertain who they need to "pitch" to and what those individuals want and need from them, a point emphasized by David Demarest. Demarest was Stanford University's vice president for public affairs, Visa International's executive vice president for corporate relations, and President George H. W. Bush's director of communications. A distinguished and successful developer of communications strategies, Demarest notes that your most important audience is not necessarily the people in front of you. For instance, when Blankfein and Hayward appeared in front of congressional committees, the senators and representatives had limited to no potential effect on their careers or probably even on the wellbeing of their companies. The audience these two CEOs were addressing was their employees and boards of directors who were looking for signals of power, strength, and reassurance that the leaders could steward their organizations through the crises each was facing.

Rob Goffee, a UK academic, and Gareth Jones, a journalist, wrote a book with a provocative title, *Why Should Anyone Be Led by You?*[24] Every day, or at least occasionally, people around you are going to ask that question: Why do you have a senior role? What gives you the right to be in a position of power and influence? Part of the answer comes from your actual job performance, from your skills and competence. But a big part of the answer derives from how you act and speak—how you show up—and if you show up in a way that inspires confidence in your capabilities.

Most normal people prefer to feel good about themselves, and that means feeling good about their employer, whose brand they carry as a consequence of their employment. People, in their motivation to feel good about themselves, want to associate with organizations—and people—who appear as if they are successful and are going to triumph during battle or another sort of struggle. People also mostly respond positively to signals of strength. Although we like to think people root for the underdog, when it comes to their own identity, they would prefer to be with the winners.

Apology, Anger, and Power

Certain emotional displays convey strength; others do not. Therefore, it is important to convey powerful emotions and avoid expressing those that signal lower status. In this regard, many people find it counterintuitive that anger is a powerful emotion and that displaying it is often a smart power move—even when, or possibly particularly when, someone has made a mistake or has been uncovered in some malfeasance. By contrast, expressing sadness or remorse and apologizing conveys much less power—and therefore should be avoided under conditions when appearing powerful and competent is important, which is more frequently than most people think.

The logic behind the argument is straightforward. Anger is associated with coercion and intimidation. Displays of anger, as examples of coercive and intimidating behavior, are typically not viewed as nice, normative, or possibly even socially acceptable. To reprise the discussion from the last chapter on rule breaking, if the powerful get to break the rules, then that heuristic association means that breaking the rules can create perceptions of power.

Similarly, if the powerful are permitted to display anger more readily than the less powerful—because displays of anger fall outside customary norms for behavior, and only the more powerful are permitted to violate social expectations—then displays of anger can create perceptions of higher status.

This logic leads to the recommendation to display anger as a way of acquiring power. This recommendation is consistent with the outcome of Blankfein's and Hayward's behaviors and what happened to each of them. Hayward's apology made him seem weaker; Blankfein's strong, unapologetic defense of Goldman made him seem stronger and raised the status of the company as well. To take another example, whenever ex–president Donald Trump was confronted on incidents ranging from the *Access Hollywood* tape (on which he boasted about grabbing women) to his response to accusations of financial misbehavior, his typical move was to double down and go on the attack. I am not saying any of this is "right"; I am only recounting the evidence on how anger—particularly when contrasted with another negative emotion, like sadness or remorse—produces higher attributions of power and status.

Social psychologist Larissa Tiedens noted that "people expressing anger are seen as dominant, strong, competent and smart" and that "people believe individuals with angry facial expressions occupy more powerful social positions than do individuals with sad facial expressions."[25] In four studies using a variety of methods, Tiedens demonstrated that "anger displays can lead to status conferral," because displaying anger conveys the appearance of competence, while exhibiting sadness conveys the impression of warmth. In a field study at a software company, Tiedens found that people who expressed anger more frequently had been promoted more, earned more, and scored higher on their managers' assessment of whether the employee should be promoted in the future. Consistent with my earlier point about getting beyond the need to be liked, Tiedens concluded: "Although anger expressions . . . result in the perception that the expresser is unlikable and cold, likability was not related to status conferral." Tiedens also coauthored a study that found that expressions of anger permitted people to claim greater value—and do better—in negotiations, because the expression of anger conveys toughness.[26]

Apology is almost the opposite of expressing anger, and is many people's default option when confronted with blame. There are three important downsides to apologizing that ought to cause someone to think very carefully before doing it. The first and most obvious downside is that apologizing "inherently associates a transgressor with wrongful behavior."[27] Responsibility for a bad outcome might have been ambiguous or contested, but once someone apologizes, the association of that person or organization with the negative action or outcomes is unambiguously established.

Second, someone who apologizes incurs psychological costs, as apology can affect people's self-perceptions. In two experiments, researchers concluded that the act of *refusing* to apologize "results in greater feeling of power/control, value integrity, and self-worth."[28] Therefore, not apologizing is consistent with people's (and organizations') desire for consistency and self-affirmation—powerful, effective, good people and organizations don't engage in wrongdoing, so they don't have anything to apologize for.

Third, and possibly most importantly, apology affects not just the social actor that apologizes, by implicating credit and blame and affecting people's feelings about themselves. Apology also affects what *others* believe about that social actor. Because apology is a low-power behavior, others will see entities that apologize as possessing less influence, status, and prestige—and this will influence those perceivers' behavior as a consequence. Thus, apologizing reduces the likelihood that the apologizer will benefit from the perception of being powerful and prestigious. As one review of the research literature on apologizing noted, "Transgressors who apologize in situations in which competence is relevant suffer a negative impact on their perceived competence . . . To the extent that thanking and apologizing are considered polite speech, research has found that the use of polite communication reflects negatively on the speaker's perceived dominance, power, and assertiveness."[29] The research on apologizing highlights the frequent trade-offs in the social perception of people between being seen as warm or competent.

Many people bring up the Tylenol example as demonstrating the usefulness of expressing remorse and apologizing. But that was a special—and unusual—case. The situation: in September 1982, three people died in the Chicago area after taking cyanide-laced Tylenol. By the time the poisoning spree was over, seven people would be dead.[30] Manufacturer Johnson & Johnson quickly recalled the product from store shelves and advertised that people should not take Tylenol until the product could be rereleased in the (now ubiquitous) tamper-evident packaging. The company's quick action assuaged public concern and Tylenol soon regained its market-dominating share of the painkiller market.

Here's the important distinction between this case and many others people confront in organizational settings: by virtually no stretch of the imagination could Johnson & Johnson, or its actions, be considered responsible for the sequence of events that killed people. Tampering with products on store shelves had not occurred before, and the company had not, by its own actions or inactions, contributed to the tragedy. This absence of agency *does not* characterize the situation facing BP, Goldman, Trump, or most other companies or individuals, who are typically far more implicated by their behaviors in the events that have occurred. When a social entity cannot separate itself from an action—to use an example from Tiedens's experimental study materials, Bill Clinton's dalliance with Monica Lewinsky—the issue of how to respond changes. Associated with the action, apology tends to lead to both a perception of weakness and to further arguments about responsibility and what should have been done to prevent the problem. By contrast, anger, and maintaining that no wrongdoing occurred as Blankfein did, eventually causes people to give up and move on as they possibly accept the image-maintaining account.

THE IMPORTANCE OF (EVEN UNWARRANTED) SELF-CONFIDENCE

Research shows that emotions—and behaviors—are contagious.[31] In medicine, there have been studies of mass psychogenic illness associated with seeing another person ill and, in a school setting, knowing that a classmate felt ill.[32] "Contagion appears to involve both biological and social processes"; it is pervasive, and people are typically unaware of the contagion even as they are experiencing it.[33] Emotions are not only contagious, they are, as noted, important. One recent review found evidence of the effects of "emotional contagion on a variety of attitudinal, cognitive, and behavioral/performance outcomes"[34] in organizational settings.

Because people want to feel proud of what they are involved with and to believe that they and their colleagues will be successful, one of a leader's most important tasks is to project confidence. When someone projects confidence, others are more likely to follow and support them—and for that matter, to hire and promote them. Moreover, if a leader projects confidence, then, following the ideas of contagion, others are likely to feel more confident and act accordingly. The importance of projecting confidence is why the first rule of power, in chapter one, was to lose the scripts, language, and (relevant to this chapter) body language that suggests anything other than self-confidence and potency, even if that confidence is unwarranted by objective reality or not what a person is feeling in the moment.

Berkeley professor Cameron Anderson and colleagues tested the idea that overconfidence helps people achieve higher social status because overconfidence signals competence.[35] In one study that used a geography knowledge task, the researchers found that not only did a person's overconfidence predict their task partner's rating of their competence and, therefore, the status accorded them, overconfidence "had as strong a relationship with partner-rated competence as did actual ability." A second study showed that the effect of overconfi-dence on perceptions of confidence and the according of status per-sisted after seven weeks, demonstrating that the phenomenon was not ephemeral. Anderson and colleagues used another experiment to ascertain the specific behavioral cues people were using to infer competence. They found that the percentage of time someone spoke; the use of a confident, factual vocal tone; providing information relevant to the problem; adopting an expansive posture; exhibiting a calm and relaxed demeanor; and offering answers were all posi-tively related to observers' perceptions of competence.

Interestingly, in this and other studies, including measures of people's personality characteristics in the analyses did not weaken the results. This finding is consistent with the argument made throughout this book that it is behaviors—ones that can be learned and adopted—that matter for the acquisition of power. It is not that personality does not matter at all, but behaviors often are more important. For instance, with respect to confidence and power, one study had participants randomly assigned to adopt an expan-sive (high-power) or closed (low-power) pose and then present a two-minute speech in a simulated job interview. People who adopted the high-power pose were more likely to be assessed as employable and have their performance rated higher.[36]

The recommendations to display confidence and anger contra-dict the conventional wisdom that advises people to display vulner-ability as a way of connecting to others, to be soft in how they show up as a way of encouraging others to come to their side to offer comfort and assistance. What to do depends on which motive is stronger in a given situation—the motive to associate with strength and success, or the motive to offer help and feel close with someone who has expressed vulnerability. Both are possible, but my read-ing of the evidence suggests that it is generally better to bet on the motive of being associated with strength and winning, and then to bask in the glory of the powerful.

One way of parsing these conflicting ideas comes from a study of self-disclosure. As the authors note, "Self-disclosure is becoming an increasingly relevant [and common] phenomenon in the work-place."[37] The authors conducted three experiments to ascertain the consequences of self-disclosing any form of weakness. They found, in the context of task-oriented relationships, "that when higher status individuals self-disclosed a weakness, it led to lower influence . . . greater perceived conflict . . . less liking . . . and less desire for a future relationship."[38] These negative effects did not occur when the individual self-disclosing weakness was a peer in terms of status. My conclusion: it is particularly important to demonstrate confidence—and competence—in task-oriented settings, especially when you hold a higher-status position and others expect you to provide leadership and reassurance.

So, yes, you can express vulnerabilities and insecurities among friends, or when you hold a position in which you are not a leader. But in high-status and task-relevant positions, you are much better off keeping any insecurities to yourself. People want to be aligned with someone who they think is going to win, to prevail, so doing anything that disabuses them of that belief is probably a mistake.

BODY LANGUAGE CAN SIGNAL POWER

In 2020, Dana Carney, a social psychologist teaching at Berkeley's Haas Business School, completed a comprehensive review of the nonverbal behaviors that signal power, status, and dominance—conceptually distinct but related constructs that manifest similarly in a person's body language.[39] Carney's review also answered a common question about nonverbal behavior: Do things differ by gender or culture? Her answer, based on the evidence to date, is "no." With respect to culture, evidence shows that nonhuman primates exhibit similar power-expressing behaviors. Furthermore, many studies of nonverbal expressions of power were conducted in other countries, demonstrating their cross-cultural generalizability. As for gender, Carney concluded that "gender does not appear to systematically interact with perceived or actual nonverbal expressions of PSDom [power, status, and dominance]." So the advice provided in this chapter appears universal.

Table 3-1 presents *some* of the nonverbal expressions of power, status, and dominance that are empirically related to these constructs. Many of the power cues are unsurprising but nonetheless important as people think about how to show up in everyday organizational life.

TABLE 3-1	NONVERBAL BEHAVIORS ACTUALLY ASSOCIATED WITH POWER, STATUS, AND DOMINANCE
More gestures	
More open body posture	
Less interpersonal distance (placing oneself closer to others)	
More controlled arm and hand gestures	
Louder voice	
More successful interruptions of others	
More speaking time	
Longer gazing time	
Higher visual dominance ratio (look + talk > look + listen)	
More disinhibited laughs	

Doubtless, people can learn how to express power nonverbally, and can become more skilled at doing so through training, coaching, and practice. An extensive research literature suggests that such efforts can be worthwhile, because nonverbal expressions of power and status have real consequences.

POWERFUL SPEECH—POWERFUL WORDS

"That words are powerful is not news to anyone in the field of marketing. The right words create an aura of desirability around a product . . . Words shape how we think."[40] Although how people look and sound are more important than what they say in the judgments others form about them, language matters, too.

Powerful speech has several characteristics. First, it is simple. Powerful speech consists of mostly one-syllable words and no complex sentence constructions with subordinate clauses. Powerful speech is easy to understand, which is one reason it is powerful. Powerful speech also does not impose large cognitive burdens on the listener, but rather draws their conclusions for them in simple, easy-to-understand words. One way of measuring how difficult it is to understand a passage (in English) employs the Flesch-Kincaid readability formula, or alternatively, the Flesch-Kincaid grade-level formula, which is inversely correlated with the readability score. Text that is easier to read means a lower grade-level equivalent.[41] The formula for the reading ease score is:

$$206.835 - 1.015 \,(\text{total words} / \text{total sentences}) - 84.6 \,(\text{total syllables} / \text{total words})$$

Short sentences with mostly monosyllabic words produce greater ease of reading (or hearing) comprehension. The grade-level formula is:

$$0.39 \,(\text{total words} / \text{total sentences}) + 11.8 \,(\text{total syllables} / \text{total words}) - 15.59$$

A second feature of powerful speech is the absence of hedging words such as "sort of" or "kind of" and few hesitations such as "um" or "er," as well as a lack of polite forms.[42] Powerful speech uses powerful words—words that evoke vivid images and arouse people's emotions—words such as "injured," "death," and "problem."

Powerful speakers make declarations instead of asking questions. Powerful speech takes into account the fact that the final words in a sentence are important—you want to end strong. Such speech uses pauses and variations in pacing for emphasis and to hold the audience's attention. Most importantly, powerful speech repeats ideas and themes. Evidence shows that "people are more likely to judge repeated statements as true compared to new statements, a phenomenon known as the illusory truth effect."[43] Two experiments demonstrated that "people were more misled by—and more confident about—claims that were repeated, regardless of how many [sources] made them."[44]

All of these ideas are illustrated in a remarkable YouTube video dissecting then-candidate Donald Trump's answer to a question on the Jimmy Kimmel late-night television show in December 2015.[45] Kimmel asked Trump if his proposed ban on Muslim immigration was un-American. Trump, like most effective presenters, answered the question he wanted rather than what was asked—much as Blankfein of Goldman Sachs answered questions about taking advantage of clients by repeatedly explaining the role of intermediaries in financial markets. In Trump's one-minute answer, 78 percent of the words are just one syllable, and the language is pitched at a fourth-grade reading level. Trump repeats the same points frequently, another characteristic of powerful speech.

Much as in the case of body language, the available evidence suggests more similarities than differences across genders. A "dual cultures" approach argues that men will use more powerful language while women will employ more powerless language. But, contrary to expectations, one study found no difference in the frequency of hedging language and no difference in the frequency of interruptions. The authors noted that "researchers have recently begun to question the necessity and/or relevance of studying sex differences in communication."[46] This conclusion does not mean there are no differences. Rather, the implication for both spoken and body language would be to try the dominant and customarily successful approach unless and until that is proven not to work.

HOW THE PERCEPTION OF POWER BECOMES REALITY

The premise of Rule 3 is that appearance—how someone shows up with both body language and spoken language—matters a great deal for how others perceive them. Those perceptions then guide others' decisions about that focal individual. The implication: master how to appear confident, attractive, and powerful in multiple ways. Because of the operation of confirmation bias and the power of first impressions, appearance (i.e., impressions created through speech and how one presents oneself) matters a great deal.

Along with extensive research evidence on the importance of appearance, the occurrence of people being taken in by those who project an image that does not conform to reality provides an endless trove of fascinating examples. Possibly the most famous is the case of Frank Abagnale,[47] whose autobiography, *Catch Me if You Can*, became an Academy Award–nominated film of the same name. During his career as a con man, Abagnale impersonated a Pan Am airline pilot, on occasion being invited into the cockpit on other airlines and being given the controls; a teaching assistant at Brigham Young University; a physician supervising interns (he stopped when he almost cost an infant his life); and an attorney. There is also the case of Christian Gerhartsreiter, better known as James Frederick Mills Clark Rockefeller, who passed himself off as a member of the Rockefeller family.[48] With that pedigree, he was able to marry Sandra Boss, "a high-earning McKinsey senior executive" who had graduated from Stanford and Harvard Business School. Boss earned all of the family income but "Rockefeller" held complete control of the family's finances.

People are fundamentally trusting. When people tell stories about their lives and careers and personas, few—maybe no one—bother to do the simple work of checking with prior subordinates, business partners, and so forth to see if the stories match the reality. People become committed to their decisions. Once people have invested either financially or emotionally in a relationship, that commitment hinders their admitting they made a mistake in judgment. Situations are ambiguous. How much power—or competence, for that matter—a person actually possesses is often difficult to discern.

All of these factors, and more, mean you should definitely follow Rule 3, and to the extent possible, appear powerful.

|R|U|L|E|

4

Build a Powerful Brand

In late 2020, Laura Chau was promoted to partner at Canaan Partners, an early-stage venture capital firm founded in 1987 that, over its history, had raised $6 billion and invested in more than thirty companies that went public. Chau recognized the importance of building a strong personal brand and she had done so by, for example, getting onto the *Forbes* 30 Under 30 list. Brand was important because, as Chau notes, "in order to succeed at a fund, you need to do the best deals possible. In order to do the best deals possible, you need to maximize your chances of actually seeing those deals. There's only so much you can do one on one, and brand felt like an incredible way of marketing, where you were able to be top of mind for people."

Chau had started a podcast called WoVen, which stands for Women Who Venture. The podcast gave her "the opportunity and the right to ask women who were very senior in their careers or founders of public companies to talk for an hour." Because most people said yes to her invitations, Chau expanded her network strategically and significantly. Moreover, her own status was enhanced through her association, in the podcasts, with high-status people. People are known partly by the company they keep. One study observed that having a prominent friend in an organization boosted an individual's reputation as a good performer.[1] Social psychologist Robert Cialdini recounted an oft-told example of this phenomenon of status by association: "At the height of his wealth and success, the financier Baron de Rothschild was petitioned for a loan by an acquaintance. Reputedly, the great man replied, 'I won't give you a loan myself, but I will walk arm-in-arm with you across the floor of the Stock Exchange, and you soon shall have willing lenders to spare.'"[2] Because status and prestige rubs off on others, people publicize their connections with successful others.[3] The implication: One way to build a powerful brand is to associate with other people and organizations that are themselves prestigious.

Chau not only used her podcast to connect with and become associated with prominent others, she also blogged regularly about topics that portrayed her as a thoughtful investor in the consumer space. She wrote a chapter for a book, a long-form thesis on social media. She commented that she was the only person to help get speaking gigs for the author's book tour. She notes that the writing made it possible for her to come across as someone founders should talk to, "instead of 'Hey, I'm this random woman, Laura, at some random venture fund, and you should talk to me about your next round of fundraising.'"

Chau began running panels of about twenty people. "I'll pick a topic I'm trying to get smarter on," she says. "Then I'll find three senior operators, and I'll ask them to be a panelist. It's a way for me to build my network of operators, and then I'll go invite the twenty founders that are building companies in this space that I want to meet. In the panel, I get all of this content from the founders and the operators who are much more expert than I am, and develop it into a blog post I can put out."

Chau also published a newsletter, called *Taking Stock*, that was opt-in for anyone she emailed with or who came to any of the events that she hosted. She uses the newsletter "as a way to stay loosely connected with the tech community." In it she shared resources, selected blog posts she wrote, and used it as a channel for feedback and nominations for people to attend her events. In 2021, Chau launched a weekly Clubhouse show called *Hot Deal Time Machine*, in which she did retrospectives on some of the hottest VC-backed deals. In her conversations with the founders and the VCs who backed them, she sought to learn from their experience. As she noted in an email to me, "It's been a fun way to build an audience on a new platform while building relationships with the guests on the show. I've also been documenting the highlights from the conversations in my newsletter."

The podcast, the newsletter, the Clubhouse show, the blogging, the panels, and the conference appearances all helped Chau develop a presence in the venture community. "By being out there and having this kind of brand, it makes it much easier for people to then say, 'Come on my podcast,' or 'Will you sit on this panel, or do this keynote?' There's sort of this circuit of speakers where I think people just look at who spoke at the last conference and then invite them to their conference. It's the ones that people tend to see. So once you're in the circuit, you can stay on the circuit, and reach a much broader audience."

Chau nicely described the many aspects of the flywheel effect of personal branding—how one thing led to another, and through these activities, someone could differentiate themselves in what would be an otherwise highly competitive space. They could stand out from the crowd. By so doing, their credibility, connections, and power would grow. That's why building a powerful personal brand is the fourth rule of power.

HAVE A NARRATIVE—AND TELL IT REPEATEDLY

A brand needs coherence. At its best and most effective, a brand brings together aspects of someone's personal and professional life in a way that makes it clear why they are uniquely qualified for some position or to found a company in a particular industry.

Tristan Walker is an African American man from a disadvantaged background. He grew up in housing projects in Queens, New York, and his father was shot dead when Walker was three. But he went on to found Walker and Company Brands, a consumer packaged-goods company focusing on serving the personal grooming-care needs of people of color—an enormous but tremendously underserved market. Walker and Company raised venture capital from firms such as Andreessen Horowitz and was acquired by Procter & Gamble in 2019. Walker was extremely effective in generating publicity for himself and his company. By 2016, when he was only thirty-two years old, he and the company had been profiled in, "among other places, *Fast Company* in an unusually long, 8,000 word piece, the *New York Times,* the *Los Angeles Times, People, Essence,* the *Wall Street Journal, Inc., Ebony,* and a host of other media."[4]

Walker has an effective narrative. As a Black man, he suffered from razor bumps when he shaved, so he had firsthand knowledge of the product need. Also as a Black man, Walker had direct experience with how few personal care products there were for people of color, and how they were often consigned to the back of stores or lower shelves. He knew that money had not been spent on product development and innovation, leaving a large, growing, and underserved market confronting products that were not leading edge. Moreover, as a Black entrepreneur, Walker could speak to the absence of people of color in the Silicon Valley start-up ecosystem—a topic that has drawn increasing attention as companies have become more interested in improving their diversity and inclusion. He was a talented and passionate advocate for and exemplar of the very phenomena his business—which hired many women and people of color to design and market products for those communities—was about.

Everyone needs a brand. Your task: think of a short (two- or three-sentence) way of describing yourself and your accomplishments that brings together your expertise, your experience (what you have done), and a way of integrating that with some aspect of your personal story. For instance, I saw a woman from Puerto Rico speak passionately in my class session on branding about the need to build a technology/knowledge-based economy to promote economic development there, and how that integrated with her own technical background and her prospective job at Thoma Bravo, a large private equity company and provider of capital founded by someone with Puerto Rican heritage. I also heard an African American physician, also getting a business degree, talk about the pressing issue of unequal access to healthcare and health outcomes, how he had experienced that growing up, and how his career trajectory incorporated ways of addressing that problem.

Once you develop a brand statement, get feedback on it from professional colleagues and friends. And then think about how you are going to get that message out into the world.

Tell Your Story Before Someone Else Does

Narratives invariably arise around people and situations. It therefore behooves you to tell your story, to craft your narrative, to create your brand identity, before others can.

In December 1997, Emory University business school professor Jeffrey Sonnenfeld was accused of vandalizing the Goizueta Business School building and then intimidated by the campus police into resigning—he was soon going to assume the deanship at Georgia Tech anyway. However, as described in a case on Sonnenfeld,[5] the deanship offer was revoked after Emory's then-president, William Chace, called his counterpart at Georgia Tech to tell him about the Sonnenfeld affair and warn him about his incoming dean.

The allegations proved specious. In July 2000, Emory settled the suit Sonnenfeld brought against the university for multiple millions of dollars, and Georgia Tech apparently paid him $1.2 million in 2009 for withdrawing its offer.[6]

In the beginning, Sonnenfeld and Emory had agreed on a story that he had resigned because of medical problems, high blood pressure in particular. Emory's Chace had agreed to not disparage Sonnenfeld, and both sides would keep quiet. Unfortunately, Chace did not keep his end of the bargain, and soon there were articles in the *New York Times*, the *Wall Street Journal*, and the *Atlanta Journal-Constitution* about the incident. For the first month or so, Sonnenfeld, embarrassed by being fired, did not tell his side of the story. Embarrassment in the face of personal setbacks is a natural but frequently unhelpful reaction, as people succumb to the just-world belief that if something bad has occurred, they must have deserved it.

Once Sonnenfeld had the supposedly incriminating video in hand, he vigorously reached out to academic and business contacts to tell his side of the story. Eventually, a broadcast entitled "The Scuffed Halls of Ivy" on the CBS program *60 Minutes* that was quite favorable to Sonnenfeld created a groundswell of support among Emory students and alumni that brought the university to the bargaining table to negotiate the eventual settlement.

One lesson from the Sonnenfeld experience confirms Mark Twain's axiom "that a lie will go halfway around the world in the time it takes the truth to put on its shoes."[7] A second lesson is the importance of getting your side of the story out early and often. Once impressions are formed, they are more difficult to change. A third lesson: Settlements on the event of someone leaving an organization frequently come with clauses that require the recipient of the money to remain silent about what occurred. The potential damage to someone's reputation and the problems caused by their being unable to tell a self-enhancing narrative can be immense. Silence is far from golden when people need to tell their version of what transpired that affected their job and career.

DEVELOP A "LOOK"

Laura Chau's parents came to the US from Vietnam. She has developed a personal style that includes advocating for herself and trying to stand out, which goes against stereotype. Taller than many Vietnamese immigrants, she intentionally wears high heels, which make her 6 feet, 1 inch tall, and intentionally dresses very stylishly. The height and clothes help make her distinctive. She commented: "For many people, I'm like, 'You're the tallest Asian woman I've ever seen.' By not being the stereotypical Asian woman who keeps her head down and works hard, I think it's helped me stand out more."

The idea of using clothes and physical appearance as part of branding is not a new or unique idea, but that does not make it any less important. Elizabeth Holmes of Theranos notoriety always wore the same black outfit as a way of signaling she did not have time to worry about what to put on. Steve Jobs also had a look (that Holmes was possibly trying to emulate). Mark Zuckerberg of Facebook was famous for his hoodies, at least for a while. Jack Dorsey, CEO of Square and ex-CEO of Twitter, has altered his appearance over the years, going from a punk style to a more buttoned-down, CEO-like look and, in spring 2020, showing up at a congressional hearing wearing an unkempt "pandemic beard." It is interesting to compare the number of articles commenting on his appearance in Washington to the number describing his testimony.

The frequent commentary on different or unusual CEO appearance makes the point that people need to think carefully about what they want to convey through their look and then do things consistent with that objective. Former San Francisco mayor and California Assembly speaker Willie Brown, the African American politician and lawyer we met earlier, who came from a poor background in Texas, ultimately dressed in (very expensive) Brioni suits and drove fancy cars. Dubbed the "best dressed man in California" by *Esquire* magazine, Brown said the secret to his success was style.[8] In a 1984 *60 Minutes* interview, Brown commented about whether he was a living piece of art. He sought to convey through his appearance—his look—that he should be taken seriously, that he had resources, and also, by standing out in the crowd, including among his fellow legislators with his clothes, that he'd developed a shrewd way of positively differentiating himself.

DO AS MANY THINGS AS POSSIBLE TO BECOME KNOWN

Once someone has a brand, a story, and a narrative that is compelling and integrates aspects of their professional (and possibly personal) life, it is essential to disseminate that narrative widely. It is also useful to match the outlets to the nature of the brand being promoted. The ways of broadcasting messages are almost endless.

Podcasts

First, there are podcasts—actually, too many of them. One way of differentiating a podcast is to get others interested in promoting it. See if you can get sponsorship, develop an interesting and unusual angle, bring on well-known guests, and mostly, persist. Jason Calacanis, author, angel investor, and event organizer—and our rule breaker from chapter two—produces the podcast *This Week in Start-ups*. He does the podcast twice a week, every week, rain or shine, except when there is some breaking news, in which case he may do an extra "emergency podcast" in which he comments on the event. Over the years, this constancy has grown his audience to more than four hundred thousand people. I sometimes say that Calacanis has enjoyed overnight success that took a decade or more to build. His podcast also benefits from a focus—in this case, on the start-up ecosystem. He interviews founders and investors, and an occasional author. Few people decline an opportunity to appear on his podcast, and the interesting founders and technology luminaries he can attract have helped the podcast—and Calacanis himself—become well known. *This Week in Startups* also has sponsors—advertisers—so Calacanis is able to monetize his reach and audience even as he continues to build his brand.

Write a Book

Calacanis, an early Uber investor, is a proponent of angel investing, and runs events to train angel investors, introduce them to one another, and bring them together with founders. To help build his brand, he wrote *Angel: How to Invest in Technology Startups—Timeless Advice from an Angel Investor Who Turned $100,000 into $100,000,000.*[9] It took him not much more than a month to complete a draft. Calacanis told me that writing that book was an incredibly shrewd use of his time as it further helped get his name out and, because the book is filled with insights and practical advice, enhanced his credibility.

If you don't want to write the book yourself, don't have the time, or lack the writing talent, hire others to help you—sometimes they are called ghostwriters. There are many such people and services. Books can help create a brand, particularly if they become well known and sell in profusion—which is one reason why sometimes people will buy copies of their own book to give away. If you write the book about yourself, you can indeed shape the narrative. In the late Lee Iacocca's autobiography,[10] there is no mention of his role in the development of the Ford Pinto, the car famous for the exploding gas tank.

While I was in Tallinn, Estonia, speaking at a conference a number of years ago, I and my spouse had a private dinner with writer John Byrne—in town speaking at a different event—and his partner. After a lot of wine, I commented to Byrne that he was at least as responsible for the mythology of success around former GE CEO Jack Welch as Welch himself. He agreed, as he had been the writer behind Welch's hagiography—pardon me, his completely truthful and complete autobiography.[11] Byrne's sentiment was not false self-promotion. In the words of a senior executive who reported directly to Welch, there were tens of thousands of other employees at General Electric, so why should Welch get so much disproportionate credit? Because he was the one with the story. The success of business autobiographies, not just commercially as books but as tools to create a narrative and a brand that burnishes their subjects' image, has led to a profusion of books about corporate leaders and entrepreneurs. Many if not most of them are incomplete in their details and obviously self-promotional, but they still succeed in creating a brand.

If even working with a ghostwriter is too time consuming, find briefer ways to get your message out. Write blogs, magazine articles, anything that can demonstrate thinking and analysis and can draw an audience. Marcelo Miranda, a Brazilian who worked in the construction and materials industry, began writing articles while in his early twenties. When some were rejected, he tried other outlets. This brand building got him featured in a leading Brazilian business magazine's issue highlighting CEOs of the future. Someone who gets into a magazine with that headline has great odds of becoming a CEO early in their career.

Speak at Conferences—or Start Your Own

Early in his career, Calacanis understood the importance of well-crafted, well-curated events with good, interesting food and drink. He now runs Launch, a venue for founders, investors, and people interested in the start-up space to get together. Prior to the coronavirus pandemic, Launch had grown to fifteen thousand people and Calacanis had cities around the world competing to host it. Again, Launch did not begin as *the* place to be for technology startups and those interested in them to connect. It grew gradually over time. One of the Calacanis "secrets" was to run numerous parallel sessions and to have people compete to get on the main stage. He also ensured that people were well prepared and the talks were interesting by insisting on seeing people's content—and providing advice on how to make it more compelling—before they arrived to talk.

Jason Calacanis now runs numerous events—Angel University, Founders' University, and other programs that bring founders and angel investors together. These events help build Calacanis's brand in the world of start-ups and angel investing. They also bring into his orbit numerous people in the start-up ecosystem who, once connected to Calacanis, can provide opportunities, information, and the learning that, over time, has made him so knowledgeable.

CULTIVATE THE MEDIA

One of the best ways to tell a story—particularly a flattering account of yourself you have developed—is to have others tell it on your behalf, because of the self-promotion dilemma.[12] On one hand, people are expected to project confidence and expertise while claiming competence. In situations such as job interviews or making a pitch, self-promotion is virtually required—how else would the target know about your wonderful qualities? On the other, there is often social disapproval and dislike for people who are seemingly boastful and "braggadocious." Research shows that if a person sings someone else's praises—even if that person has a financial incentive to do so, such as an agent—many of the downsides of self-promotion disappear. The media can be excellent advocates, and that is true even if the media are indirectly (or directly) paid to tell a favorable story. There are now sections explicitly labeled as advertising—but looking like regular content—in magazines and newspapers. Moreover, as master builder Robert Moses demonstrated, you can cultivate the media by having them attend events with good food and wine and lots of access to people that they want to meet.

Possibly the best way to cultivate the media is to provide easy and ready access to yourself—be willing to do personal interviews—which helps the media do their jobs with less effort. In today's world, most media people are operating with tight deadlines and limited budgets while working long hours. Making it easier for them to write about you and what you are doing activates the norm of reciprocity while giving them an attractive, easy-to-cover subject.

J. J. McCorvey, the *Fast Company* writer who penned the extremely long profile of Tristan Walker, commented on Walker's accessibility: "As soon as I reached out, he started to set up all of these opportunities for me to observe him in his element and really get to know him and his friends and his family. I've written many stories about many people, but that was still the most access I've ever had to a subject, ever, and that's a reporter's dream."[13]

Nuria Chinchilla, a professor at IESE, the business school in Barcelona, is well known for her writing, consulting, and policy work in the area of work–family conciliation. She is the director of the International Center on Work and Family at the school. In addition to getting herself known, she has tirelessly sought to bring prominence to the topic of work–family integration and to women in the workplace. Her fame comes partly from her writing but also from her ability to draw notice to that writing and other activities. Early on, Chinchilla recognized the importance of media coverage and took steps to obtain it.

"First, she was accessible, taking journalists' calls, often doing interviews as soon as they were requested, and being willing to work with the journalists' schedules and deadlines . . . Chinchilla was willing and able to be a public figure—a role that requires a lot of time and energy."[14]

Chinchilla provided journalists access to the conferences she organized and the senior leaders who attended. She shared data from her research with them. And she focused on building relationships with the media from the beginning:

It began when we had the first meeting only for women human resource managers in 2001. The day before the meeting, someone

*called and said that they had heard I'd done research . . . and could
they have an interview. And what I did was to say, "Okay. You
are in Madrid. Tomorrow, I will be in Madrid. Why don't you
come to the meeting . . . at the IESE campus? You can not only
do my interview, but you can interview all the women there. You
can attend all the sessions, have lunch with us, and then you can
write whatever you want." And from then, everyone is asking to
have an interview. I am doing my interviews mostly by phone in
the car, in my office, from home. Every time, every hour. I am . . .
providing a good service to the person who wants to have an interview. So this is why the television and radios and newspapers are
happy with me, and then they come back.[15]*

Many corporate leaders believe they do not need to cultivate the
media. They don't want to spend the time or the effort—that's why
they have marketing and public relations people. Alex Constanti-
nople, a public relations executive who had worked with Tristan
Walker, noted that many executives thought they did not need a
personal brand, but that Walker held the opposite view. Mark Suster, an entrepreneur and venture capitalist, had worked at Sales-
force with Marc Benioff, its founder and CEO. He said that Benioff
"understands the importance of the media, and he writes personal
notes to journalists. He takes all the calls himself." That may be one
reason why Benioff seems to enjoy more favorable coverage than
many of his technology peers.

STAND OUT BY BEING APPROPRIATELY CONTROVERSIAL

In addition to building relationships with media people and making their jobs easier, another part of brand building entails becoming newsworthy. In today's world of pursuing clicks and eyeballs,
getting attention—being newsworthy—mostly entails being controversial. Once again, Jason Calacanis has much to teach us.

In the 1980s, Calacanis started a publication called *Cyber Surfer.* When a dispute with the owner/backer caused it to fold, he started the *Silicon Alley Reporter* to cover the New York technology scene. Five years later, the magazine, built off his credit cards, was generating $12 million a year in revenue. In an effort to get the magazine more visibility, during its first year of operation Calacanis started the Silicon Alley 100, the hundred most important people or companies in the area. Of his desire to rank the contenders, he said:

> *My team is desperately trying to get me not to rank the list because they are afraid it will upset people. And I said, "That's precisely why we're going to rank it." So who is number one? It's obviously DoubleClick; they have more money, a product, more employees. So I say, "Great, they're number two" . . . I want everybody to be talking about this list, and why the person who's number one is more important than them. So I picked Esther Dyson. She's a woman, Bill Gates calls her for advice . . . she's a tech visionary. For the next seven, eight years, my entire life was consumed with people lobbying me to figure out where they were on the list for the next year.[16]*

If the Calacanis strategy seems familiar, it should. John Byrne drew attention to the first ranking of business schools published by *BusinessWeek* in 1988 by selecting as the top-rated school not Harvard or Stanford or Wharton or MIT, but Northwestern, which at the time was not nearly as prominent. An unobvious choice, a controversial position, draws attention.

People who knew Calacanis commented that his hero was Howard Stern, the shock jock, author, actor, and producer. When Travis Kalanick got into trouble for Uber's "bro" culture, Calacanis came to his vigorous defense on CNBC's "Squawk Alley." Calacanis was always willing to say what he thought, which made him a desirable guest and why CNBC had been after him to become a regular with his own show. At a party, Michael Ovitz, former president of Disney and cofounder of Creative Artists Agency, told Calacanis that he loved him on CNBC. Why? "You always tell the truth. Whatever anybody's thinking, you just come out and say it. You take a side and you defend people and you don't split hairs."[17]

LEVERAGE PRESTIGIOUS AFFILIATIONS WHENEVER POSSIBLE

Sadiq Gillani was hired as the head of strategy for the prominent airline Lufthansa when he was thirty-two years old, becoming the youngest senior vice president ever appointed. Gillani was chosen for that position by the CEO at the time, Christoph Franz, even though he did not speak a word of German and was going to join a very traditional, very German organization. In January 2022, Gillani joined the supervisory board of Condor, the second-largest airline in Germany, as a sort of vice chairman, and also joined Attestor Capital, the new owners of Condor, as a senior advisor for their airline and travel investments. Gillani's career nicely illustrates how he used his position at Lufthansa to extend his brand.

When Gillani joined Lufthansa, the former head of Seabury Consulting (a boutique consulting firm serving the airline industry, where Gillani had worked following business school and had become a partner) told him that he had a great platform and to leverage it to build exposure and prominence. Gillani took that advice, and it paid dividends for him in boosting his visibility and brand in the airline industry.

For instance, Lufthansa was, not surprisingly, a member of the World Economic Forum, but had not been that active in the organization. Gillani described how he leveraged his position in Lufthansa to substantially enhance his network:

> I went to Davos as part of the Lufthansa delegation, learned about the YGL [Young Global Leader] community, and decided to try to become part of it. One of the requirements was that the CEO of your company, which was my boss, had to write a recommendation

for you . . . I was accepted into the program. I had become the company representative of Lufthansa to the WEF and was also able to join their Global Future Council for Travel. This is about 20 people from across the world who help design the agenda of the WEF when it comes to travel and mobility.[18]

Gillani was invited to Stanford to give a talk to the Travel and Hospitality Club. The talk went well, he met the associate dean in charge of the MBA program, and soon he was co-teaching a compressed (two-week) class on the travel industry at Stanford. He used his WEF connections to get speakers for the class. The students appreciated seeing senior figures from the industry, and the prestigious executives themselves loved being invited to lecture at Stanford.

Gillani's prominent role in airline strategy and his connections to the World Economic Forum resulted in an invitation to give a TED talk, which drew considerable interest, generating some 135,000 views. Gillani noted that when he was introduced to the organizer of TED in Germany, he suggested doing the first-ever TED talk on the airline industry.

Gillani commented that the various brand-boosting activities built on one another. "Because of his prominent role at Lufthansa and his admission to the YGL group, *Capital* magazine named him as one of the 40 under 40 executives in Germany. The *Financial Times* anointed him as one of the top 100 OUTstanding executives [Gillani is gay] and top 100 Ethnic Minority business leaders."[19] Gillani was accessible for interviews not just for internal Lufthansa publications but also for many business publications, and received a reasonable amount of media coverage.

What worked for Gillani can work for other people, too. If you have a job at a prestigious organization, go beyond just adding it to your résumé and public profile. Leverage that association to obtain connections to other high-status positions and organizations and build even more personal brand equity.

TAKE CREDIT FOR YOUR WORK

Part of brand building and creating a positive reputation is ensuring that you get credit for your work. That entails being willing to tell your story and eschewing any false sense of modesty or the belief that your work will speak for itself. Your bosses and colleagues are busy and often focused on their own objectives. Don't expect them to necessarily notice or credit your accomplishments.

Deborah Liu, formerly vice president for Marketplace at Facebook, a board member at Intuit, and recently appointed CEO of Ancestry.com, had worked at Facebook for more than eleven years. An engineer with patents to her name and prior experience at PayPal, Liu used to think her performance would speak for itself. As she told me, she went to Facebook to build what would eventually become its games business and Facebook Credits. The business she had helped build was so significant—about 15 percent of total revenue—that it was a separate item in the earnings report and in the S-1 when the company went public. She commented, "When we finished, we had never really talked about it and no one cared. A couple of people from the team left the company and everyone else went on to do other things."

With Liu's career not progressing as well as she thought it should, and being frustrated with the lack of recognition for her and her team's work, she availed herself of some executive coaching—it was through her coach that I met her. The coaching convinced Liu that she needed to tell her story and also the story of the teams she was leading so they could get credit for their work, something that she had not done in the past.

When Liu returned from maternity leave, she started a new project that was called Mobile App Install Ads, which enabled Facebook to recommend apps to download. "This was 2012 when we were getting killed for not solving mobile monetization, as we barely had ads on mobile," she said. "Our team was asked to address this. At the time, we were a brand advertising company, and we were building the first direct response advertising vertical from a team not in Ads."

Liu had learned to let others know what she and her team were doing. She explained:

> I told everyone I met, "We're going to solve mobile monetization, and here's how we're going to do it."
>
> Our core team was like five people—three engineers, a borrowed data scientist, and myself. But I posted about what we were doing everywhere internally. I wrote decks and strategies.
>
> I went to Mark [Zuckerberg] and I pitched him on it. I did everything I could to get the work out because we had so few resources. Everybody wanted to help. Partnerships leads from Europe said, "I'll take this product to market for you." And they went and met with developers and explained how it worked and set them up to test this new type of ads. It was about telling the story over and over. Not only did everyone know about this product, but then people started spreading the word for us. The executives mentioned the product in an earnings call. By telling the story and connecting it to the biggest problem in the company, we got dozens of people to help us in their spare time. People wanted to be part of something that was going to address an acute need. They heard the story and wanted to be part of writing it. Even to this day, many years after we gave up the product, the story is told of a small team that did something incredible at a time that was critical to the company. Today, the product is a leader in its space, but it is small relative to the scale of Facebook. But the narrative has become a touchpoint that inspired other teams that want to do something big.

Deborah Liu wound up getting more credit for a smaller product achievement than she did for something of greater economic significance, because she had created and told a narrative—repeatedly—that possessed all of the elements of what people want to hear.

Saint Joseph College professor Richard Halstead observes that "the story of the hero's journey has been told and retold . . . for cen turies."[20] It captures the "strength and perseverance of the human spirit," speaking to the challenges people face and the possibility of personal transformation and triumph. The story's structure is often the same: a person faces an unexpected setback, which becomes an opportunity for learning and personal transformation. Having learned an important lesson, the individual reengages in a way that produces success, thereby validating the learning and development they have experienced.

Therefore, Deborah Liu's story illustrates a second important lesson beyond the importance of telling others about what you and your team are doing, and repeating that story frequently. To build a lasting brand, you also must craft the narrative in a way consistent with the hero's journey, so that people are more likely to remember it and, more importantly, embrace its inspirational message.

BECOME WILLING TO TELL YOUR STORY

Many people, particularly women or those raised in cultures that inculcate the value of modesty, are reluctant to engage in what feels like self-promotion. The problem is that if you don't tell your story, you cannot be sure that anyone else will, either, or whether others in the organization will see what you have accomplished.

One way to overcome the reluctance to engage in personal branding and self-advocacy is to reframe what this activity entails and means. Deborah Liu talks about how she inspired another person to do this:

> I was doing a talk at this event and we were talking about self-evaluation, and this woman said, "I'm just really not good at self-promotion." And I said, "Do you see what you just did there? If you treat your self-evaluation as self-promotion, you are not going to talk about the work that you're doing. You're not going to

do it justice. If you call it helping your manager understand the impact that you have, if you call it helping your team get the recognition it deserves, would you see it differently?" And she said, "You're right. I've been thinking about this all wrong."

This small reframe can help people understand the necessity— and the importance—of telling their story, and the story of their colleagues, while making them more comfortable in undertaking the critical task of building their brand.

One final thought. The idea of self-promotion, of personal branding, seems to contradict the recommendation of Jim Collins in his book *Good to Great* about Level 5 leaders, who have modesty coupled with fierce determination.[21] I note three things. First, Collins studied effective leadership behavior *once people had attained* CEO positions. As he and I once discussed, the behaviors required to ascend hierarchies may differ greatly from the optimal behaviors for someone ensconced in power. Second, by Collins's own numbers, Level 5 leaders were extremely scarce, about fourteen out of more than fourteen hundred. Studying exceptional behavior is interesting but possibly not as useful for guiding the behaviors of most people. And third, recent research shows that hiding success, although common in everyday life as people have been told to be modest, actually has interpersonal costs.[22] That is because others feel that they have been treated in a paternalistic fashion by those who hide their success, which leads the others to feel insulted.

|R|U|L|E|
5

Network Relentlessly

OMID KORDESTANI, A PERSIAN AMERICAN WITH an electrical engineering degree from San Jose State University and an MBA, was Google employee number 11 and the first business person it hired when it was still a tiny company. From 1999 to 2009, he was Google's senior vice president of worldwide sales and field operations.[1] He left with a net worth of over $2 billion. When Google wanted him back for a short stint in 2014, they paid him $130 million for about a year's work.[2] Today Kordestani is a member of Twitter's board of directors after serving as its executive chair.

Some years ago, Kordestani gave a talk at Stanford during which, in response to a question, he said that my class on power was the most important he had taken at the business school. Besides driving up the popularity of the course, the comment made me curious. What had he found so useful? I reached out and we had breakfast. He told me the following story, a tale that nicely illustrates the theme of this chapter about the importance of social relationships and networking for career success.

Kordestani said that as someone with an immigrant background and an engineering education, he had eschewed any form of organizational politicking, despite having taken my class, believing that the quality of a person's work spoke for itself and that people should be modest and self-effacing. Not embracing the class material, Kordestani did not particularly stand out as a student—I hardly remember him from that time. When he graduated in 1991, he first went back to Hewlett-Packard and then to a couple of startups, Go and 3DO, that did not do great.

In the mid-1990s Kordestani joined Netscape, the famous browser company cofounded by Marc Andreessen, just as the internet was taking off. His work in marketing and business development there was good, but Kordestani didn't think his career was progressing as well as it should. So, he told me, he took my class's message—that performance was often not that important and social relationships and sponsorship mattered more—to the maximum and radically changed how he spent his time. Kordestani decided to devote less time to the technical aspects of his job and more to building relationships and interacting with people both inside and outside of Netscape, so he could be more noticeable and known. After all, if no one knows or notices someone, their good work will not help them much because it will be invisible.

Netscape was not that big a company, so in addition to spending time with its senior leaders, Kordestani built a network throughout the broader Silicon Valley ecosystem. This was the beginning of popular interest in the internet and the debut of web browsers, so there was much to talk about and learn. Of course, this networking made his excellent technical work and his intelligence and interpersonal skills more widely visible. Moreover, building relationships was completely consistent with the tasks of marketing and business development that constituted his job.

When the Google team decided to bring in a business person in the late 1990s to complement the tiny start-up group working on search, they did what Google is prone to do: rely on data to make their decision. Their comprehensive search of the Silicon Valley talent pool consistently uncovered one name on almost every list of technology-oriented business people—Omid Kordestani's—and he became a candidate. Even then, Google was highly selective and did multiple interviews with candidates. One of Kordestani's interviews began around four in the afternoon and was still going on as dinnertime approached. Kordestani, who in addition to being smart is also very interpersonally skilled, suggested that the group go out to dinner—and he would pay for the meal. In a more informal atmosphere, his great ability to relate to people and his business smarts stood out, as there was less pressure. As he said, the return on investment on that dinner, which resulted in his being hired as employee number 11, was essentially incalculable.

Or to take another example, consider Ross Walker, the youngest person ever to serve on the Stanford University board of trustees and today the founder of real estate investment firm Hawkins Way Capital, with $1 billion in assets under management. Walker argues that "people are the name of the game."[3] While a student, Walker organized interesting social events for fellow students. He used his summer between his first and second year to work, for free—he turned down payment when it was offered at the end of his tenure—for Chip Conley, an alum who had founded a successful hotel chain. In school, Walker spent time finding a place to work where he would learn and possibly develop a good relationship with a mentor. He got a job with Lew Wolff, a well-known real estate developer who had interests in hotel chains and sports teams, and who became an important mentor and one of Walker's early backers. At graduation, Walker became an investor in and befriended the operators of high-end nightclubs and venues in Los Angeles so he could offer exciting and exclusive evenings to people he wanted to meet. Real estate development essentially entails matching projects with investment capital, and getting a project off the ground often involves interacting with local zoning authorities and suppliers of services ranging from construction to marketing. In all of this activity, knowing a lot of qualified people, and being able to build relationships successfully, are critical skills.

Keith Ferrazzi, the marketing guru and rule breaker we met in chapter two, wrote a book on networking titled *Never Eat Alone.*[4] The success of his marketing consulting and speaking firm, Ferrazzi Greenlight, depends on his ability to attract talent to work with him and customers who know about him and the company. He needs to know people and, more importantly, he needs to be known. When hiring someone for consulting or speaking, it is obviously necessary to know of the person or firm's existence and have a positive image of them, so Ferrazzi takes relationship building seriously.

When he turned forty, Ferrazzi had friends organize birthday parties in seven different cities, all of which he attended. At the party in Palo Alto, about a third of the people I randomly talked to didn't know Ferrazzi personally prior to that evening. Ferrazzi used the occasion to keep building his network while reconnecting with people he already knew. Ferrazzi has stated that his goal of leaving a legacy, of making an impact in the world, requires him to enlist the help of others, because he cannot accomplish what he wants by himself. Simply put, social relationships matter for getting things done, in organizations or in society more broadly.

The old saying "it's not what you know but who you know" has at least some truth. Who you know, and how many people you know, matters for your influence and for your career. Therefore, Rule 5 of the seven rules of power is to network relentlessly. Your networking may not permit you to hit the proverbial lottery like Omid Kordestani did, or to write best-selling books and build a consulting firm like Keith Ferrazzi, or to become a successful real estate investor like Ross Walker. But networking and building social relationships will, as much evidence demonstrates, build power and accelerate your career. This chapter presents the evidence for these statements and some guidance on how to network—and how to build effective networks—more efficiently.

SPEND ENOUGH TIME INTERACTING WITH (USEFUL) PEOPLE

Humans are social creatures, so most people do spend some of their free time interacting with others. The problem from the standpoint of Rule 5 is that much of this interaction is with family and friends, not with bosses, colleagues from work, or others who might be professionally useful.

For instance, a study using American Time Use Survey diary data found that on average people spent 112.9 minutes—just over two hours—per day socializing, but only 9 of those minutes were socializing with colleagues.[5] Another survey of more than twelve thousand business professionals found that individuals who said that networking played a role in their success spent an average of 6.3 hours per week on networking, while those who maintained that networking did not play a role in their success networked just two hours a week or less. The article's conclusion: people should spend eight to ten hours a week building professional relationships because "the secret to getting more business through networking is . . . spending more time doing it!"[6]

Why People Don't Spend Enough Time Building Social Relationships

Almost everyone recognizes the importance of professional networking—building social connections with instrumentally useful others—to their work and careers. The fact that they don't engage in this activity sufficiently often begs the question of why.

This query has several answers, and they are far from mutually exclusive. Daniel Kahneman, the psychologist who won the Nobel Prize in Economics, and colleagues developed a survey method for assessing daily life experiences. They found that socializing was rated second only to intimate relations as the most positive activity people engaged in during a day.[7] However, they also found that the specific interaction partners mattered a lot for people's positive or negative evaluation of their time spent socializing. Interactions with friends, relatives, and spouses were experienced much more positively than were interactions with coworkers, bosses, or clients and customers. Therefore, one reason that people don't engage in professionally useful networking is that they don't find the experience particularly enjoyable.

Moreover, research shows that people may see professional networking as a less moral activity because in some sense it entails building relationships for someone's personal advancement. Many people seemingly hold the belief that it is inappropriate to interact with others for instrumental reasons.

If people do something they perceive as less moral, they can feel dirty as a result, as assessed not just by their self-expressed attitudes but also by how much they value products associated with cleansing. In a field study at a law firm, researchers Casciaro, Gino, and Kouchaki found that people felt professional networking was dirty. However, higher-power people were less likely to feel that way, which may be one reason those individuals had more power. And regardless of people's feelings, the data showed that networking was related to professional success.[8] In a series of experiments, the authors demonstrated the relationship between professional networking and feeling dirty. So a second reason why people don't network as much as they should is they see it as using others for their own purposes and therefore somewhat immoral, leaving them feeling dirty when they engage in this nonetheless career-boosting activity.

Another issue is that because interpersonal relationships and friendships are important, people are reluctant to use work-based friendships to address career or work problems. For instance, in a study of the use of networking to find a job, people who "asked others for job-related advice or help . . . worried about straining interpersonal relationships or felt embarrassed if they looked bad."[9] With people spending more time at work, and work a central part of life for many, numerous and important social relationships are forged in the workplace. But mixing professional interests with these more spontaneous friendship relations poses dilemmas and feels uncomfortable for many people.

Even when people do engage in networking, they often see it as a task to be done, not as a skill to be developed. When I interviewed him for a case about Ross Walker, Chip Conley, the hotel entrepreneur, author, and former Airbnb executive, made this insightful comment about the implications of seeing networking as a task versus as a skill:

> When people think of it [networking] as a task, it's something you do and then you sort of deposit it away. You know, you don't think, when you're actually taking the trash out, what's the set of elements I could do that would make me better at it. I think a lot of people think of networking as a task. And I think that he's [Ross Walker's] taken it to a level of skill. And when you are trying to build a skill, you are much more apt to be strategic or analytical about how you get better at it.[10]

Networking and Career Outcomes

Most people believe that professional networking for instrumental reasons, albeit possibly uncomfortable or unnatural, results in better career outcomes. Those intuitions about the importance of networking are correct and backed by several research studies. The increasingly social, interdependent, knowledge- and skill-based aspects of work make the willingness and ability to build social ties ever more important.

For example, a longitudinal field study of 112 employees assessing career success after three years found that "networking was the most robust predictor of career success." Another longitudinal study observed an effect of networking on both concurrent salary and the growth rate of salary over time as well as a relationship between networking and career satisfaction.[11] A study of 510 employees at a professional services firm found that networking was positively related to both in-role and extra-role performance.[12] Yet another study examining 191 employees in a wide range of occupations found that networking ability dominated other aspects of political skill in its ability to explain career outcomes including total compensation, promotions, and career and life satisfaction.[13]

Systematic reviews of the networking literature also demonstrate the importance of networking for career outcomes. Florida State professor Gerald Ferris has conducted extensive research on the importance of political skill, research previously mentioned in this book. In a study of which political skill dimensions were the most important for career outcomes, such as work productivity, career success, personal reputation, and job satisfaction, networking ability was among the most important.[14] Another synthesis of the research on networking in organizations concluded that networking "leads to increased visibility and power, job performance, organizational access to strategic information, and career success."[15]

Social relationships are critical for career success and developing the capacity to get things done. Yet because many people do not enjoy networking and find it uncomfortable to be strategic in their social interactions, it is imperative that they be intentional in *how* they spend their time—and in choosing the people *with whom* they spend it.

THE CASE OF JON LEVY

Because networking seems like work and can make people feel dirty, most people spend insufficient time on social relationships with professionally useful others. But from the right perspective and implemented in the right way, networking—meeting and interacting with new and interesting people—can be a wonderful experience and even a good career in itself. No one better illustrates the upside of networking, and how to do it with style, than Jon Levy.

I first came across Levy when I read a *New York Times* article[16] describing an influencers' dinner in his New York apartment. He brought twelve or so people from a variety of backgrounds together to cook a simple meal—and wash the dishes—with the proviso that no one could tell others what they did or who they were until after dinner, when people had to guess the identities of their co-attendees. Levy noted that when people can't talk about their work, it creates an additional level of novelty and intrigue, putting people on equal footing and reducing their tendency toward arrogance because they do not know the status of their interaction partners.

Jonathan Daves, a managing director at WRT Ventures in Los Angeles and someone who has worked with both my online and on-campus power classes, knew Levy and had been to a dinner. Did I want to meet Levy, Daves asked? Absolutely. Soon I was in the beautiful San Francisco apartment of Levy's brother (who is director of portfolio research at Moody's Analytics), talking to Jon in advance of my first dinner. We connected through our mutual interest in social science and how the world works—it is easy to connect with Levy because he is intellectually curious—and the following is what I learned from interviewing him as well as from personal observation.

Levy is smart and interested in social science—he has just published his second book, *You're Invited*, with HarperCollins—and it turns out we share the same editor, a point of connection and similarity that is important in the relationship-building process. His parents, both Israeli, although not highly educated, are extremely talented: his father is a painter and sculptor, and his mother is a composer and conductor.

Levy graduated from New York University in 2002 having studied computer science, math, and economics. During college he worked for Cutco Cutlery, a direct sales company, and he ran an office for them after he graduated, becoming one of their most successful salespeople. Levy worked at a large New York catering company and did digital strategy for Rodale Inc., the company that owned *Men's Health, Women's Health,* and *Runner's World,* among other titles. He was doing fine in his work, but nothing exceptional—as he said, he was not a person he'd have invited to one of his influencers' dinners.

Then Levy attended a seminar around 2008 or 2009 where the leader noted the importance of the people we surround ourselves with in our lives. Levy became determined to spend time among the "most exceptional people in our culture because I wanted to gain their knowledge and their habits to improve the quality of my life." From that beginning came his subsequent trajectory.

Levy's description of how he landed on the dinner format is insightful, and contains principles that *everyone* can apply as they think about bringing people into their lives. First, he thought about doing phone calls to meet and learn from people, but he realized that no one wanted another phone call, particularly from someone they did not know. Recognizing that for influential, successful people, everyone was after them and wanted something from them, Levy noted that what he would do "had to be generous, because I can't just be another person asking for something." He needed to lower their defenses so they could actually connect with each other, and with him.

Levy knew that when people invested effort—in a person, in an activity—they cared about that entity more, because they see it as someone or some activity worthy of their effort. An example of how escalating commitment and the expenditure of effort builds value is a phenomenon that has been called the IKEA effect, after the furniture company whose products customers have to partially assemble.[17] In studies, researchers found that when participants folded origami, built Lego sets, or assembled plain black IKEA storage boxes, people valued their creations comparably to those of experts and expected others to agree with them.

In addition, Levy knew that whatever he did had to be novel, because novelty causes people to explore and seek to understand their new experience. He also understood that "if you can curate an environment with high-profile people, they'll go out of their way to be there," an example being Davos, the site of the World Economic Forum. Levy argued that the "most desired human emotion or experiences" entail wonder. All told, he understood that he needed something generous, novel, well curated, and at least occasionally able to trigger wonder.

Thus was born the influencers' dinners, and a career for Levy of organizing experiences for companies. Today Levy has a whole team of researchers to track down potential guests and a review board to vet them. Prior to the pandemic, he was doing five dinners a month in three or four cities. Since COVID, the ability to do events virtually has permitted Levy to expand their size while being on the road less.

A final, important lesson from Jon Levy. He noted:

Our influence is a by-product of who we're connected to, how much they trust us, and the sense of community that we share . . . To create a sense of community, you need membership. There has to be a clear line delineating inside and out, and maybe a common language, a shared history, a feeling of influence . . . I would argue that the methodology is highly scalable, but the influencers' dinner is intentionally not.

Jon Levy, Keith Ferrazzi, and Ross Walker are very different people. What they all have in common is one essential thing: an intentionality in how they have structured their social worlds that far exceeds that of most people. But that level of thoughtfulness doesn't have to be so rare. With effort (because this all involves work), study of the relevant social science, and reflection on their own experiences, people can do their versions of building a social world that provides both pleasure and power.

FOUR FUNDAMENTAL NETWORKING PRINCIPLES

Four principles are important for ascertaining how to make networking efforts as efficient and effective as possible.

Pursue Your "Weak Ties"

In the early 1970s, economic sociologist Mark Granovetter published a study of the job-finding process. Examining the job searches of 282 people in the Boston area, Granovetter observed that most jobs were found not through formal channels such as job applications or responding to advertisements, but through the informal information supplied by social ties.[18] The surprising finding was that the ties that were most useful for finding a job were not the strong ties with family, friends, and close work colleagues, but instead the ties with casual acquaintances—so-called weak ties.[19]

The straightforward intuition behind this finding: people to whom one is strongly tied are likely to be strongly tied to each other, and therefore share mostly the same information, contacts, and perspectives. People to whom one is weakly tied are more likely to tap into different sources and social circles, and are therefore more likely to be able to provide non-redundant information and contacts. This non-redundant information has higher value because of its greater novelty. Research also shows that weak ties are associated with greater creativity,[20] again because of their connection to more diverse perspectives, ideas, and sources of information.

How can weak ties be helpful? *Any* tie is better than cold calling—hence the phrase, "warm introduction." People prefer others who are similar, who are part of their social circle—who constitute the "us" and are part of their in-group. It turns out that it does not take profound, deep social connections to be more "us" than "them," or to create a sense of shared social identity. For instance, when Ross Walker began raising money for his real estate fund, two of his significant early investors came through weak ties—one a connection to a college roommate that Walker had not been in close contact with for years. Often such casual, weak ties are sufficient to provide credibility and make the difference between closing the deal or not.

Research done since Granovetter's study has examined the relationship between weak ties and emotional and psychological wellbeing. A study of 242 undergraduate college students found that the more classmates they interacted with, the happier they were and greater their feelings of belongingness. Focusing specifically on weak ties and also including a sample of community adults replicated these findings: "Interactions with people on the periphery of our social network may contribute to our social and emotional well-being."[21]

The straightforward message of weak ties' importance: don't spend too much time with people who are close. Instead, ensure that you are meeting a wide variety of people in a wide variety of organizations and industries. You never know when one of them will have information important to your job performance or career prospects.

Become a Broker

University of Chicago sociologist Ronald Burt, whom I first got to know when we were both on Berkeley's faculty in the 1970s, is justly famous for his analyses of the benefits to people who, to use his term, "bridge structural holes"—in other words, provide brokerage. What do brokers do? They bring together parties who could profitably benefit from interacting with or knowing each other. Real estate brokers connect buyers and sellers of property. Investment bankers connect people with capital to invest with those who need capital, and mergers and acquisitions bankers connect buyers of businesses with parties interested in selling them. Venture capitalists connect individuals who have technology and business plans to people with the capital to help bring those plans into fruition. Executive search firms connect companies with positions to fill with potential candidates. You get the point.

The people and organizations who connect those who can benefit from being connected profit from this activity and the service they provide. The underlying intuition about how and why brokers create and accumulate social capital is straightforward: in general, notes Burt, "opinion and behavior are more homogeneous within than between groups so people connected across groups are more familiar with alternative ways of thinking and behaving. Brokerage across the structural holes between groups provides a vision of options otherwise unseen, which is the mechanism by which brokerage becomes social capital."[22]

In a study of one electronics firm, Burt found that outcomes including compensation, positive performance evaluations, promotions, and having good ideas were all more likely to accrue to people whose networks bridged structural holes.[23] Reviews of an ever-growing literature have consistently confirmed these findings.[24]

The practical implication: network structure matters. People's careers—and their job performance—are enhanced if they can find positions or jobs where they can perform brokerage and bridge structural holes—connecting units, people, or organizations that would mutually benefit from being exposed to different ideas, information, opportunities, and resources.

You might ask, can someone benefit if they don't want to or for some reason can't obtain beneficial network positions? Although this question has not been answered generally, with respect to brokerage it has been answered—in the negative. Ronald Burt conducted a study in which he found that "brokerage benefits are dramatically concentrated in the immediate network around a person," and that secondhand brokerage—"moving information between people to whom one is only connected indirectly—often has little or no value."[25] The message: networking cannot be subcontracted to others. To obtain the benefits of networks and structural position, a person has to be in a favorable spot—and must do the work to get there themselves.

Be Central

Zia Yusuf, a Pakistani graduate of Macalester College in Minnesota with master's degrees from Georgetown in foreign affairs and Harvard Business School, began his career post-university at Goldman Sachs. Then, in January 2000, he joined SAP, the prominent German software company, as a board assistant to Hasso Plattner, its cofounder and leader. After leading SAP Markets, a marketplace organization that was closed down, Yusuf was tapped to lead a newly created internal strategy group with the mandate to bring in external talent and perspectives, manage SAP's relationships with external consulting firms, and drive internal strategy and analysis.[26]

By 2008, Yusuf was going to be promoted to the executive committee of SAP. This despite being a Pakistani in a very German company, a non-engineer in an engineering-oriented organization, and someone who had never worked in product or even sales. How to explain his success?

Yusuf was smart, with an unusual ability to read situations and build relationships with people. He also had another source of power. As the head of strategy, he had great exposure to the senior executive team, attending many executive board meetings where he would present his group's analyses. He also interacted with numerous people and units across the organization. In a diagram of the communication structure inside SAP's senior ranks, strategy—Zia Yusuf—was in a central position, as the nature of its work entailed acquiring and transmitting information across the organization, leaving the unit and Yusuf with profound informational advantages.

As it turns out, instead of accepting the promotion, Yusuf left to become CEO of a technology start-up in the business of managing parking resources, and subsequently joined the Boston Consulting

Group as a partner. Yet research confirms the lessons from his SAP success. A field study of the effects of network centrality on the exercise of power in technical and administrative innovations demonstrated the importance of centrality, net of individual characteristics, particularly on administrative power.[27] Another study found that people in more central positions were more likely to engage in interpersonal citizenship behavior inside workplaces.[28] A large meta-analysis of the effects of communication network structure confirmed the importance of centrality for the behavior of people in the networks.[29]

Centrality affects visibility. More people will know and know about people who are more central, and that visibility will often work to those people's advantage for becoming the focal point for information and opportunities. Centrality also affects access to information. The first network studies demonstrated that people in central positions saw more information—because more communication flowed through them—and had greater direct contact with more people. The implication: when people evaluate jobs and roles, one dimension they should account for is the centrality that will accrue to them from occupying that job or position. Other things being equal, choose more central jobs.

Create Value for Others

Last, be sure to create value for others—or why would people want to be connected to you? Sometimes this idea is described as being generous. I would describe it slightly differently: as putting yourself in the other's place, having some empathetic understanding of where they are coming from and what challenges they face, so that you can provide help reasonably easily and effectively. Help taps into the norm of reciprocity—the idea that favors create an obligation for some form of repayment later on.[30] Help also binds people together through liking; people like those who help them more than those that don't. And providing value to others through social relationships transforms networking from something dirty or transactional to something viewed much more positively by everyone, including the networker. It is now more about serving and being of service to others.

Two implications follow. First, as Ross Walker has told my class, if you want to get value from your connection to another, don't make that other do your thinking for you. In other words, to the extent that you have a specific request for some specific help for a specific and sensible reason, others can quickly ascertain whether and how they will connect you to resources that might be helpful. If you show up with a more general request, such as helping you think through career options, the response won't be as favorable because the request is too general and untargeted.

Second, offering help to others actually helps build your power. If you can connect people to others in useful ways, you have implicitly demonstrated your centrality and value just by being able to make those connections. The more connections you make, the more people come to see you as a well-connected (translation: powerful) individual. Thus, helping others builds your own reputation even as it provides a service of real value—the very definition of win-win.

NETWORKING TIME MANAGEMENT

Networking takes time, and there are always other things to do— being with friends and family, making decisions, doing the technical aspects of your job. Therefore, it is important to be as efficient as possible with the time you devote to building social relationships.

Technology can help. People are used to "checking in" and updating others using email and social networking sites such as LinkedIn and Facebook. They're probably not as good as a more personal connection, but as a way of keeping in touch, better than nothing. You can also use various relationship management software to keep track of who you have been in touch with and which contacts are growing stale and need renewal. It is important to recognize that sustaining a relationship, particularly a weak tie, does not require intense or deep connections. Casual updates, sharing an interesting article about a topic of mutual interest, or letting people know you are thinking about them is often sufficient. Keith Ferrazzi stayed connected to his high school roommate by calling him every year on his birthday.

Xavier Kochhar from Los Angeles describes himself on LinkedIn as a master of video and data. He has worked for AT&T and Warner Media and founded organizations in the digital media space. I interviewed him as part of preparing my case study of Ross Walker. Along with noting that it was my job to convince people that they could do what Walker had done, even though many people were not willing to expend the time and effort to do so, he had two comments relevant to making networking more efficient. First, he argued that people needed to balance investing in building a social network with harvesting the results of those efforts:

> Any master connector will eventually hit a point where they will have to make a very tough but very important decision: how to balance network growth with generating utility from the network . . . Most people are good at one or the other or sometimes neither. It is the extremely rare person who has properly solved the network growth to network value extraction ratio. But those few that have rise to the top very fast—and stay there.

Second, Kochhar noted how Walker and many other successful people allocated their time in a particular way: they spend more time with those on the periphery than at the center, more time on people distant than on those who were close. He noted:

> I call it the "social acquisition paradox" . . . The further someone is from the center, the harder the person in the center works for them . . . It's because the connector is trying to draw them in . . . those closest to the connector . . . often get less compared to those farther away . . . why would you want to double down on somebody who's already in?

Balancing network growth with network value extraction, and spending more time on people being cultivated than those who are already part of one's social circle, are two other ways—along with leveraging technology and maybe building a staff (after all, hiring help is often not that expensive)—to become more time efficient in networking.

We end this chapter with a practical exercise for you to do, an admonition for you to implement its results, and some statistics that tell you why. Consider how you spend your time, maybe by looking at your calendar, asking others, or some combination. Are you devoting enough time to building social relationships and engaging in social interactions? And with whom are you spending your time? Are you building brokerage relationships—connecting people or organizations who could benefit from such connections? Are you associating often enough with high-status others? Are you spending your time in professionally useful ways, at least on occasion?

Believe it or not, people can learn about how to see social capital—and that learning translates into many career advantages. In an internal Raytheon study, Ronald Burt compared people who went through a training program that taught them networking principles with those who did not go through such a program, and with executives who had been nominated for the program (i.e., were considered skilled and with potential) but who had not yet taken it. He found that program graduates were "36–42% more likely to receive top performance evaluations, 43–72% more likely to be promoted . . . and 42–74% more likely to be retained by the company."[31] Networking, like other power skills, can be taught and learned. It is important to master this rule of power.

|R|U|L|E|
6

Use Your Power

WHEN VICE PRESIDENT LYNDON JOHNSON ASSUMED the presidency following John Kennedy's assassination on November 22, 1963, he appointed Jack Valenti as a White House aide that night. Valenti, who subsequently served for thirty-eight years as head of the Motion Picture Association of America, said that Johnson immediately decided to use his power vigorously.

On the flight back from Dallas on Air Force One, reported Valenti, Johnson sat with three people in his bedroom for six or seven hours. During that time, he sketched out the Great Society, which included Medicare, Head Start, highway beautification, the National Endowment for the Arts, the National Endowment for the Humanities, the creation of the Cabinet department of Health, Education, and Welfare (later split into two separate departments), the war on poverty, the Civil Rights Act of 1964, and much more. Valenti recalled Johnson saying:

> *"Now that I've got the power, I aim to use it," and he said, "I'm going to pass that Civil Rights Bill which has been locked up too long. I'm going to pass an Education Bill which is going to make it possible for every boy and girl . . . to get all the education they can take . . . Number three . . . I'm going to pass Truman's Medical Insurance Plan," which today is Medicare. And he went on and on.*[1]

Johnson understood three things. First, when a person is new in a position, they have time, before their opponents get a chance to coalesce, and while the incumbent is in sort of a honeymoon period, to get a lot done. This includes actions that will help perpetuate their power on the basis of their accomplishments and the changes they make to institutionalize their power.

Second, enemies tend to last longer and keep grudges more than friends remember favors. This means that, practically speaking, the longer someone is in a position, the more opposition they will accumulate, the more precarious their position will become, and the more difficult it will be to get things done. Thus, because their time in a powerful role will be limited, people need to act quickly to accomplish their agenda.

The increasingly politicized nature of organizations means that the tenure of leaders has shortened. A 2019 article noted that "last year 17.5 percent of the CEOs of the world's largest 2,500 companies left their posts—representing the highest rate of departures that PwC . . . has tallied" since it began studying CEO tenure.[2] In 2000, the average CEO could expect to be in their job for eight years; over the 2010s, that declined to just five years. Big-city school superintendents last an average of five and a half years.[3] Hospital CEO tenure also averages about five years. "Since 2012, the turnover rate was 17% or higher which is the longest period of time the rate has been so high."[4] What is true for CEOs is true for many other senior roles in organizations of all sizes and types.

Third, and the principal theme of this chapter, is the idea that power is not some scarce, limited resource that becomes depleted by being used. Instead, the more someone uses their power to get things done—including structuring the world around them and changing who works with and for them in ways that support themselves and their objectives—the more power they will have. Using power signals that you have it, and because people are attracted to power, the more you use your power and demonstrate that you are powerful, the more allies you will accumulate. Therefore, Rule 6 is to use the power one has, maybe even using more than people think you have. Using power effectively is more likely to perpetuate it than to exhaust it.

USE POWER QUICKLY TO GET THINGS DONE

On January 3, 2011, Amir Dan Rubin became CEO of Stanford Hospital and Clinics (later known as Stanford Healthcare). Rubin was an outsider, having been the chief operating officer (COO) at UCLA Medical Center, and faced the challenge inherent in outside succession of gaining acceptability and credibility. When he arrived, Stanford's emergency department was in the fifth percentile nationally and its patient satisfaction scores were in the 40s. His predecessor, who was retiring after eight years, had been focused on solving severe budgetary issues, and hospital staff considered her not very visible.[5]

Rubin moved quickly to install what came to be known as the Stanford Operating System with a strategy of focusing on improving the patient experience. Following the principles of the quality movement, Rubin had departments develop relevant measures of how they were doing and made performance against those measures visible with graphs and charts everywhere, even in his office.

He made it clear that whatever the performance was in the current year, he expected improvement the next year. Rubin instituted numerous large meetings of managers and trainings on topics ranging from how to hire, to better ways of onboarding new people, to effectively recognizing and rewarding employees. No aspect of operations was to be left to chance; instead, the organization would use—and diffuse—best practices. Rubin insisted that everyone on the leadership team, including those without patient-facing responsibilities such as finance and purchasing, make rounds in groups throughout the hospital to see patients and staff in the late afternoon or early evening twice a month—and that included him.

Rubin also took action to address the small but disproportionately annoying problems that exist in almost every organization. For instance, he arranged to have a leaky roof over the vascular surgery offices fixed—and this in a building that was going to be replaced in a couple of years by a new hospital that was under construction, so the repair money would be "wasted" on a building slated for disuse. He instituted valet parking, something that the vascular surgery department and others wanted, as many of the hospital's patients came long distances for treatment. With initially free valet parking, patients could more easily navigate the disruption of new-hospital construction without adding the stress of trying to find parking to that of the medical visit.

As a result of the Stanford Operating System, overall hospital performance improved dramatically along several dimensions: financially (operating profit increased some 300 percent in four years, while revenues grew about 50 percent); clinically, with much-reduced errors and hospital-acquired infections; and in terms of patient satisfaction, which soon reached the ninetieth percentile. Rubin had put a new team in place—not intentionally, he claims—which led to substantial turnover not just in the C-suite but two and three levels down, as newly installed leaders replaced direct reports who would not be able to substantially enhance operational effectiveness. Rubin's visibility to the entire staff—through meetings and trainings he attended, hiring leadership several levels down, instilling his new team with his operating philosophy, and spending time with hospital trustees—all created power. Now, both staff and board members could be proud of the hospital being named the best in California and among the top fifteen in the US by *US News & World Report*.[6]

These results, along with the personnel and operational changes necessary to produce them, helped build Rubin's power—and his already high national visibility. When he left Stanford, it was for a highly senior position at Optum, part of UnitedHealth Group. About eighteen months after that, he became CEO of a growing chain of primary care clinics, OneMedical. OneMedical went public (ONEM) in early 2021 and currently has a market capitalization of $4 billion. I use the case I wrote on Amir Rubin to illustrate principles of building power as an outsider—and doing so quickly.

What works in the private sector works elsewhere as well and for the same reasons. Making positive change by using power encourages people to come over to your side and enhances your performance before people can do anything to sabotage your efforts. In November 1995, Rudy Crew became chancellor of New York City's schools under the administration of Rudy Giuliani. Crew had come from a school district in Tacoma, Washington, with half as many students as New York had teachers. People thought he would not understand New York City politics (even though he had been born there). As he told my class, while people were standing down, to use the military term, sort of napping and underestimating him, he moved forcefully. As one article described:

In his first year and a half on the job, he studied the system and searched for weaknesses. Then last fall he delivered a series of reforms like so many punches. First, he took over several chronically failing schools and placed them into what he called "the chancellor's district" . . . Next, he implemented his major literacy campaign. After that, he released budget report cards on every school in the city, which gave parents a wealth of information . . .

Then Crew provided a detailed budget for the Board of Education and, in the process, proved that central headquarters was no longer the money sinkhole that many critics had claimed. After that, Crew unveiled a plan to overhaul the city's byzantine special-education program and announced that he was finding funds to restore arts education to all schools. In December, he announced that New York would be the first urban system in the country to adopt citywide the New National Standards . . . Then, in the knockout punch, the state legislature passed the governance law, which reversed some 30 years of educational practice in the city by making district superintendents directly accountable to the Chancellor . . . Suddenly Crew was the city's most politically successful chancellor in a quarter-century and the country's most important urban educator.[7]

Making changes quickly and improving outcomes increases a leader's power because it provides a rationale for others to support them. And using power is often necessary, as organizations are generally beset with varying degrees and forms of inertia, so improvement requires altering existing ways of doing things. Existing people and processes usually have some investment in the status quo, so it requires power to accomplish improvements. Successfully using power to make changes increases the incumbent's power, while waiting to use power or not using it at all leaves the status quo in place, thereby reducing power. Power, used effectively, increases its wielder's power.

USE POWER TO BRING IN SUPPORTERS AND MOVE OUT OPPONENTS

When Gary Loveman became COO (and later CEO) of what was then Harrah's Entertainment, he moved out some senior people, including the head of marketing, who had recently won the Chairman's Award for his performance. The chief financial officer, Loveman's principal rival for the CEO job, eventually left to become CEO of a competitor. Loveman's plan for the ultimately very successful transformation at Caesars Entertainment (the company's name after Harrah's purchased the corporation that owned Caesars Palace and other casino hotels) depended on the use of advanced analytics, which required a new set of skills. Loveman brought in people with those skills, because, he noted, he did not have the time to train existing personnel in the new, analytically based capabilities.

Such personnel replacement is common for new leaders in organizations of all types, who typically bring in their own teams to help them lead organizational transformations. At Stanford Healthcare, within a couple of years of Amir Dan Rubin's arrival, virtually all of the senior leadership and department heads and leaders, even three levels down, were new. Not everyone from the old regime was up for meeting Rubin's new, higher performance expectations, and few people like to have their underperformance displayed in charts and graphs. Later, at OneMedical, Rubin recruited people he's worked with before. Likewise, wherever Rudy Crew has gone as superintendent—New York, Miami—he has brought in some of his own people to fill senior roles and implement his school improvement efforts. In 1999, when Kent Thiry became CEO of kidney dialysis provider DaVita, then called Total Renal Care, he had already "reached out to a set of people who had been with him in his previous dialysis venture, people whom he trusted, liked and respected."[8] He recruited Harlan Cleaver to be his chief technology officer, Doug Vlechk to lead the organizational change and culture building efforts, and Joe Mello to be COO.

Enhancing performance and making change requires people with the requisite skills and also alignment with the vision. Loveman has said that the prior chief marketing officer at Harrah's had made his career taking pictures of crab legs and beautiful venues. Loveman's strategy instead called for using analytics to identify the most profitable customers and then building greater levels of customer loyalty by treating the people who made the cash register ring differentially based on their economic value to the enterprise. The previous incumbent did not have—nor could he likely develop— the quantitative chops to handle the new tasks.

When hiring allies to help a newly installed outsider lead an organization, it is useful to work with people who understand one's communication and operating style, which makes everything move more quickly and efficiently. It is also important, maybe essential, to have everyone on the same page. People you have worked with before are less likely to resist your strategy and improvement initiatives—or to sabotage them.

Replacing people, then, has two positive effects on your power. First, it staffs the organization with people who have aligned perspectives and the competence to execute effectively, and that increased performance will help cement your power. And second, it provides you with allies in situations that are often challenging and politically fraught.

Strategic Outplacement

Research confirms the intuition that succession often leads to turnover among the people who report to the new leader.[9] Turnover in the management team is particularly evident in the case of outside succession and if prior performance was lower.[10] It is not only in politics where leaders bring in "their" team; this happens in organizations of all kinds, including businesses. The problem becomes, then, how do leaders remove people in the context of labor laws that often restrict their freedom of action, even in parts of the US and more so elsewhere in industrialized countries where people cannot be fired without cause? Moreover, setting aside legal and regulatory issues, how can one rid oneself of opponents and rivals in ways that appear to be more benign and socially acceptable?

I have already described one way to do this: couch the turnover as part of a performance improvement effort in which new skills and a commitment to better results are required—a situation that is often true while also being politically useful. Another way is to send one's "problems" to a different and maybe even better position elsewhere, removing them from the immediate environment where they can cause difficulties while earning their gratitude for helping their careers. I have come to call this method "strategic outplacement." Here is a classic example, albeit from the world of politics.

Willie Brown, former San Francisco mayor and California Assembly speaker, was an amazingly skillful politician. After winning a bitter speakership contest in 1980, he used a state redistricting plan that gave the Democrats a huge advantage to provide "an honorable way for his strongest Democratic opponents to leave the Assembly for seats in Congress in the 1982 elections":[11]

Among those who availed themselves of the . . . escape hatch to Congress were Howard Berman [Brown's principal rival for the speakership in 1980] . . . and Brown's chief rivals, Mel Levine and Rich Lehman . . . Other Democratic Assembly rivals, like Wadie Deddeh of San Diego, got safe seats in the state Senate . . . The Republicans never quite understood how rewarding Brown's Democratic rivals helped solidify his power by removing them as threats.[12]

Employing strategic outplacement requires that the person not act on their natural feelings of resentment or anger toward rivals or sources of other difficulties. This ability to act strategically and dispassionately is a rare but important quality that few people possess. Here's an example.

On May 22, 1991, Dr. Frances Conley resigned as professor of neurosurgery at Stanford Medical School. Conley had been the first woman to have a surgical internship at Stanford Hospital, the first female faculty member in any medical department at Stanford, and in 1982 had become the first female tenured professor of neurosurgery at a US medical school.[13] Although she had suffered various forms of harassment for years, the precipitating event for her resignation was Dean David Korn's appointment of Gerald Silverberg to the role of department chair despite Silverberg's sexist behavior.

Conley's action drew the attention of the major newspapers[14] and morning news shows and sparked an outcry among students in the medical school, where female students complained about ongoing sexist behavior and where Conley was soon seen as a hero for drawing public attention to the problem. Later that summer, Conley, who had received a master's in management from Stanford business school (which is where I first met her), rescinded her resignation to remain on the faculty, where she would have more leverage to accomplish change in the treatment of female students, faculty, and staff members.

Conley's prominence, along with her research and clinical skills and her administrative capabilities (she later became chief of staff at the Palo Alto Veterans Health Care system and chair of Stanford Medical School's faculty senate), brought her numerous speaking engagements and inquiries about administrative positions ranging from department chair to dean in the years following her resignation. When I interviewed David Korn for a case I wrote on the situation, he told me that he had known that the best way forward for him was to provide Conley with glowing recommendations so she would be offered a job and thus be gone from Stanford. But, he confessed, his antipathy for her—she had committed, after all, the cardinal sin of insubordination in not complying with Korn's wishes—always got in his way, and he invariably inveighed against her to the people calling to do background checks. This behavior caused Conley to remain on the faculty, and her staying and keeping the issue of sexism in the medical school led to internal and external investigations and finally the end of Korn's deanship. The story ably illustrates the potential for using strategic outplacement as long as one exercises the emotional maturity and pragmatic, unemotional mindset required to do so.

USE POWER TO SIGNAL HOW MUCH POWER YOU HAVE—AND YOUR WILLINGNESS TO USE IT

One of the recurring themes in this book, and particularly in the next chapter when we consider how power insulates people from punishment for past actions taken to acquire power, is that people want to associate with winners and success. Therefore, it is important to demonstrate that the leader will remain in their role and will constitute a force to be reckoned with—thereby demonstrating toughness and a willingness to do what it takes to keep one's position and do whatever they want. In this regard, I am reminded of the famous quote from Machiavelli's *The Prince* on the usefulness of fear for projecting power: "It is much safer to be feared than loved because . . . love is preserved by the link of obligation which, owing to the baseness of men, is broken at every opportunity for their advantage, but fear preserves you by a dread of punishment which never fails."[15] Machiavelli also appropriately noted that the first responsibility of a leader was to hold on to their position, because if they lost it, they would no longer be able to get much accomplished.

Robert Moses, whom we met in chapter two on rule breaking, "played a larger role in shaping the physical environment of New York state than any other figure in the 20th century,"[16] and influenced urban design and construction worldwide. His displays of power helped bring him more power because people came over to his side when they saw he was willing to literally bulldoze the opposition.

In 1936, Moses wanted to mothball a ferry that crossed the East River so he could tear down the ferryhouse and use the land for the East River Drive approach to the Triborough Bridge. The seventeen hundred people who used the ferry, which ran every twenty minutes, wanted to keep it operating as long as possible. Mayor LaGuardia said the ferry service could not be stopped for the sixty days construction would require. But Moses wanted to display his unstoppable power and didn't want to wait sixty days. As described in Robert Caro's Pulitzer-winning biography of Moses:

*He [Moses] ordered the contractor building the East River Drive
approach . . . to procure two barges and install a pile driver on one
and a wrecking crane on the other. When they were ready . . . he
waited until the Rockaway [the ferry] had . . . pulled away from
Manhattan . . . and then, without warning, ordered the barges
towed into the ferry slip and lashed together . . . so that the Rockaway . . . would have no place to dock when it returned. And he
ordered the pile driver and the crane to pound and pull the slip
to pieces. Attacking also from the land side, he dispatched crews
of workmen to tear up York Avenue's cobblestones in front of the
ferryhouse to cut off all access to the terminal by land.*[17]

The mayor called the police to stop the razing, but of course, by
then it was too late as the building was destroyed. This pattern of
behavior—doing what he wanted and needed to do, regardless of
opposition or sometimes even the law—made Moses a formidable
figure but led to overconfidence. In a struggle to tear down a playground to expand parking for the Tavern on the Green restaurant in
Central Park, Moses overplayed his hand, but the description of his
thinking—and his power—is instructive:

*Local protest over a park "improvement" may have been a new
story . . . but it was an old one to Moses—old and boring. Ever
since he had become Park Commissioner he had kept such protest to a minimum by keeping the "improvements" secret, so
that, often, before the neighborhood concerned knew there was
an improvement planned, it was already under way . . . On the
seismograph on which Moses recorded public tremors, in fact, the
Tavern-on-the-Green protest had barely registered. Twenty-three
mothers? He had just finished evicting hundreds of mothers
rather than shift a section of the Cross-Bronx Expressway a single
block! He was at that very moment in the process of displacing
five thousand mothers for Manhattantown, four thousand for
Lincoln Center!*[18]

Because Moses was willing to wield his power and do so aggressively—his most famous quotation is "Those who can, build. Those who can't, criticize"[19]—people, including politicians, other public officials, and owners of construction companies, saw him, correctly, as someone who could get things accomplished. His effectiveness at creating public works—he "built 13 bridges, 416 miles of parkways, 658 playgrounds, and 150,000 housing units, spending $150 billion in today's dollars,"[20] mostly in New York City—attracted people to him and helped keep him in power for forty-four years. People were willing to overlook his abrasive personality and his disdain for any authority other than his own because he could be tough, very tough, on people he saw as standing in his way.

Because perception helps create reality, wielding power in ways that demonstrate power, doing things that signal power, helps to ensure that power will be perpetuated.

USE POWER TO ESTABLISH STRUCTURES THAT PERPETUATE POWER

When Steve Jobs was forced out of Apple (to which he successfully returned, ruling over the company until his death), every founder in Silicon Valley apparently learned an important lesson about the tenuousness of power regardless of their presumed success. Many founders then put this fear—or realization—of possible removal to rest by setting up dual-class voting structures so that their shares would have governance rights (e.g., to select directors or consider mergers) disproportionately greater than the fraction of the company they owned would allow. Although these arrangements violate the principle of one share, one vote, and are therefore anathema to proponents of good corporate governance, they are widely used.

Some examples: Facebook's Mark Zuckerberg has shares that provide him ten votes for each share, giving him almost 60 percent of the voting power and rendering him essentially untouchable.

At News Corporation, Rupert Murdoch and his family have *all* of the voting power. Google has three classes of stock, providing the founders more than a majority of voting power. When Snapchat's parent, Snap, went public, the public shares had no voting rights at all. Other companies with dual-class shares include Groupon, Zynga, Alibaba, Shaw Communications (where again the public shareholders have no voting power), and Uber—had Travis Kalanick wanted to, he could have held on to power and not left the company. In 2017, 19 percent of the companies that went public on US exchanges had at least two classes of stock with differential voting powers; in 2005, it was just 1 percent.[21] The reason that companies can get away with structures that institutionalize founders' power through dual-class stock is that when "hot" companies are contemplating a public offering, they exploit investors' desire to get in on the deal to structure its terms to the advantage of incumbent leaders.

Another structural way of entrenching power is for one person to hold both the role of CEO and chair of the board of directors. Although this arrangement is less common than it once was—in 2007 and 2008 the proportion of companies with combined roles was above 60 percent—it remains high, with 45.6 percent of companies having one person hold both roles as recently as 2018.[22]

A third strategy for entrenching power is to ensure that there are no likely successors in place. One of the reasons that Jack Valenti was head of the Motion Picture Association of America for thirty-eight years was that he did a good job representing the industry—and he ensured that there was never a likely successor in place. Sidney Sheinberg, the former head of MCA/Universal, said:

> *"Jack never groomed even a theoretical successor—there never was a guy or woman who for a moment you thought could succeed him" . . . Levinson [Lawrence Levinson, an attorney who had worked at Paramount in government relations] said of Valenti that "he learned from the Master . . . It was the Johnson model of not having a strong No. 2 man. I would say to him . . . "You're president for life."*[23]

I once served on the board of a publicly traded portable ultrasound company. I noticed that whenever the board was effusive in its praise of a senior executive other than the CEO, that executive was soon gone under one pretext or the other. I commented to one of my fellow board members that the best way to keep talent in the organization would probably be not to overly praise them to the point that they might appear to be a plausible successor for the CEO role. Removing likely alternatives as a method for holding on to power is an old, and often effective, strategy.

Fourth, it is possible to hold multiple overlapping roles that make it difficult for rivals to get rid of someone because that person would need to be removed from multiple positions in order to remove their power—a much more difficult task. Robert Moses exemplifies this principle. At one point, Moses held twelve positions simultaneously, including "New York City Parks Commissioner, head of the State Parks Council, head of the State Power Commission and chairman of the Triborough Bridge and Tunnel Authority."[24] Moses mastered the use of public authorities that could issue bonds and collect revenues such as tolls, which increased his independence from the legislative appropriations process and provided yet another source of his enduring power.

By demonstrating power and the willingness to use it, by accomplishing things, and by establishing structures that institutionalize power, the use of power becomes self-reinforcing. As the examples in this chapter illustrate, not all use of power will be met with unalloyed approval, so leaders need to be willing to incur some level of social disapproval—recall that the first rule of power is not being overly concerned with being liked. Moreover, there is inevitably some risk in scheming to remove rivals and establish rules that help perpetuate power. However, because most people are usually averse to conflict, it is surprising how much one can accomplish by seizing the initiative. And because people tend to sidle up to power once it is established, foes can become friends, enemies neutralized, and power secured.

|R|U|L|E|
7

Success Excuses (Almost) Everything

Why This Is the Most Important Rule of All

The greatest perquisite the rich and powerful in this country possess is the ability to commit crimes with impunity.
—Jesse Eisinger, ProPublica reporter and Pulitzer Prize–winning author, personal email

Victors don't just write history; they rewrite history.
—Safi Bahcall, *Loonshots*[1]

SOUTH CAROLINA SENATOR LINDSEY GRAHAM ONCE called ex-president Donald Trump, before he took office, "a race-baiting, xenophobic bigot."[2] Graham was one of many Republicans who vigorously criticized Trump during the 2016 campaign as he "called the future president a 'kook,' 'crazy' and 'unfit for office,' among other things."[3] Yet in 2019, when Mark Leibovich wrote a profile on Graham for the *New York Times Sunday Magazine*, he asked Graham, who by that time had become one of Trump's most vehement, vocal, and loyal supporters, to explain the change. Graham's response has much to say about how achieving a position of power changes things, including someone's relationships with other people:

> *"Well, O.K., from my point of view, if you know anything about me, it'd be odd not to do this," he [Graham] said. I asked what "this" was. "'This'" Graham said, "is to try to be relevant." Politics, he explained, was the art of what works and what brings desired outcomes. "I've got an opportunity up here working with the president to get some really good outcomes for the country," he told me. An outcome of particular interest to Graham at the moment is getting re-elected to a fourth Senate term in South Carolina, where Trump owns commanding approval numbers.[4]*

It was not just Graham who accommodated Trump as the Republican party marched "headlong . . . into the far reaches of Trumpism."[5] Nor are changes in people's perceptions of others once they have achieved power and renown confined to the realm of politics. Lists of most-admired CEOs often include people who have backdated stock options (Steve Jobs), had relationships outside of marriage with underlings (Bill Gates), violated SEC orders (Elon Musk), had to flee countries to avoid prosecution (Carlos Ghosn), been forced from their jobs over a scandal (John Browne of BP), and were criticized over the work environment for both blue-collar and white-collar employees (Jeff Bezos). The desire to be close to power, almost regardless of how achieved or the wielder's current behavior, implies that people should not fret too much about their path to power. Once power is achieved, everything—well, almost everything most of the time—will be all right.

PEOPLE WORRY ABOUT THE CONSEQUENCES OF FOLLOWING THE RULES OF POWER

Students often describe my course on power as a "forcing function," in that it forces them—sometimes outside their comfort zone—to embark, at least temporarily, on a path to power. Even inviting people to speak in the class has an effect. Deborah Liu, the former senior executive at Facebook who is now CEO of Ancestry, told me that knowing she was coming to the class to talk made her more ambitious in what she was willing to do, so she would have more to talk about.

Many of the self-reflective projects that I use in the course have been described briefly in the relevant chapters of this book. For instance, I ask people to develop a brand that succinctly captures who they are and what they stand for. Class members determine the people to whom they should be connected and then strategize how to forge those relationships, often expanding their network during the course. I ask people to become more comfortable with pushing the rules, and to lose the scripts and self-descriptions that hold them back. I encourage them to practice acting and speaking in a more powerful fashion. These exercises "force" people to think strategically about forging a path to power.

This forcing function, along with providing people the knowledge—and the confidence—that they can actually expand their power, are some of the more important aspects of my teaching. Knowledge and confidence, turned into action by having people develop relevant behaviors, create and change people's actions and get them unstuck. This stimulus to action is important because many people remain fundamentally ambivalent about seeking power, notwithstanding the general acknowledgment that, in most social organizations, power is necessary to get things done.

This ambivalence about seeking power arises partly from the worries people have about acquiring power and what it might take to do so. For instance, people worry about the process of obtaining power. What if their actions offend people? What if they stress the bounds of propriety and push the envelope of social norms?

People also worry about the consequences of becoming more powerful. What if, in their rise to power, they create enemies and rivals of the people they outcompete? What if, as is almost inevitable, their success provokes jealousy and resentment? What if the nail that stands out does actually get hammered down, and, like the legend of Icarus, having flown too close to the sun, they fall?

Power as a Motive

Worries aside, many people seek power because it is a strong motivational force. Studies going back decades have found that the strength of power motivation predicts holding a position of power and is associated with displaying artifacts that signal prestige and status. Moreover, research shows that there is no reliable gender difference in the strength of the power motive between women and men.[6] However, not everyone is equally motivated by power, and power is something that at least some people abjure, possibly because it signals too much ambition, overly individualistic, selfish behavior, or excessive Machiavellianism. To be clear, power and influence are almost invariably necessary to get things done and change lives, organizations, and the world. Yet to help rationalize their reluctance to pursue power, people find ways of worrying about the steps they may need to take to acquire it and what will happen to them upon doing so.

My response to these concerns is that people should downplay their importance or relevance, because power itself makes many problems, including what someone did to acquire that power, mostly disappear—the heart of Rule 7. Moreover, in order to fall from power, you must have achieved it in the first place, so we can worry about your losing power after you have it.

Of course, holding a high-level position often generates jealousy. People envy success and status, not powerlessness. But power also increases others' desire to be close to and associate with the power holder. Having power increases people's visibility and the scrutiny of their actions, thereby increasing the likelihood of their facing criticism as a result of the greater attention. But power also increases people's willingness to overlook a powerful person's misdeeds, which is the argument of this chapter.

People's power increases the likelihood of others trying to unseat them. There are invariably more contests for positions at the top of the pyramid than for spaces at the bottom. Power, however, also increases the number of supporters someone has, because people are attracted to and by power and want to be in the orbit of the powerful. There is more competition for positions at the top of the hierarchy, but there are also more individuals who want to be allied with those on or going to the top. If you are going to be successful in acquiring power, you probably will have to break some rules—that was, after all, the theme of chapter two. Yet rule breaking also helps to create power. In short, acquiring and holding power does unleash some social dynamics that are inimical to the power holder.

However, possessing power and status, occupying a dominant position, also calls forth social processes that act to perpetuate someone's power. In fact, the evidence suggests that you needn't worry too much about what you did to acquire power—or, for that matter, falling from power. That is because many organizational and social dynamics perpetuate advantage once acquired rather than diminish it. This chapter describes why its title is customarily true: power and success will generally lead others to forget or forgive what you did to attain them.

Simply put, Rule 7 is that power and its associated prestige excuse almost everything. Its implications are straightforward: your task is to acquire power, and once you have it, you will probably keep it. This chapter will, I hope, convince you of the validity of this insight.

MOST SOCIAL PROCESSES PRODUCE CONSISTENCY OR AMPLIFICATION OF ADVANTAGE, NOT CHANGE

Many people see—or want to see—the organizational world in homeostatic terms. Much as a thermostat keeps room temperature reasonably constant, organizational and social processes act to maintain balance, redress injustices, and ensure high levels of organizational performance. Try to rise up too high, too fast, and you will be brought down. This explains sayings like Japan's "the nail that sticks out gets hammered down,"[7] and Australia's tall-poppy syndrome, where poppies that grow too high get cut down (to size) and humility and modesty are valued.[8] In the homeostatic view, if you violate social norms, you will be sanctioned, so that the normative order can be maintained. Break the law or violate rules and you will face punishment, again to maintain the inviolability of the rules and laws for the wellbeing of the collective. Underperform, or misuse resources, and you will face penalties, as social collectivities enforce rules to ensure their continued survival. Homeostatic processes restore justice and order, punishment of wrongdoing enforces the social norms, and sanctions for poor performance all operate in ways that facilitate the operation—indeed, the survival—of social systems.

Although these are nice ideas, and are even occasionally true, organizational and social processes mostly amplify existing advantages and perpetuate power and status, instead of balancing or curtailing them. In that sense, organizational behavior is mostly consistent with the "Matthew Effect." According to the New International Version, the Gospel of St. Matthew states: "For whoever has will be given more, and they will have an abundance. Whoever does not have, even what they have will be taken from them" (Matthew

25:29).[9] Research on the Matthew Effect was originally undertaken by sociologist Robert Merton to describe the awarding of status and recognition in science. Merton observed that bestowal of credit was in some sense unfair, in that more prominent, prestigious scientists received disproportionate recognition for subsequent scholarly contributions, even if those contributions were jointly produced.

In essence, the Matthew Effect describes a process of cumulative advantage. "Initial comparative advantages of trained capacity, structural location and available resources make for successive increments of advantage such that the gaps between the haves and the have-nots in science (as in other domains of social life) widen."[10] Ascribed markers of social status, such as gender, affect the credit authors receive for published work. For instance, research published by women is cited less frequently, although this effect is smaller in subfields and disciplines characterized by higher diversity.[11] Higher-status coauthors receive more credit for publications, which of course means that any given coauthored study helps the reputation of the higher-status individual more, granting them further reputational advantage. A review of empirical data revealed that the operation of cumulative advantage where success breeds more success was widespread, and not just in the awarding of status in science. For instance, in social networks, the idea of preferential attachment means that "more connected nodes are destined to acquire many more links in the future."[12]

Cumulative advantage arises from many social forces. The more powerful and successful someone is, the more likely it will be that talented people will want to work with them—and the ability to attract more and better talent increases the chances of subsequent success. Likewise, the more powerful and successful someone is, the greater the odds that others will want to invest in and with them. This advantage in attracting resources increases the likelihood of future success and higher performance. Confirmation bias—the tendency for perception to confirm preexisting beliefs—suggests that once someone has enjoyed success, that individual will be perceived as successful again in the future, regardless of objective measures of results. Research shows that people pay more attention to confirming information, remember information that fits their perceptions more readily, and selectively forget discrepant information.[13] Cognitive processes of attention and memory and a preference for consistency in beliefs thus act to reinforce initial advantage.

While cumulative advantage partly explains why power, once obtained, is so durable, it does not provide a full psychological account of why power often endures even in the face of subsequent failure, demonstrated incompetence, and unethical or even illegal behavior. To explain the endurance of power that makes Rule 7 likely to hold in multiple situations, we need to delve further into the mechanisms that allow various forms of misbehavior to be excused.

An Alternative Perspective: The Costs of Power and Status

Before arguing that power is often self-perpetuating, I first want to acknowledge that the idea that power excuses misdeeds is not an obvious, or unambiguously supported, position. Here are some mechanisms that might account for why power leads to *more severe* sanctioning and a more probable downfall for the powerful.

University of North Carolina professor Alison Fragale and her colleagues argued that more powerful actors were perceived to have a greater degree of agency and intentionality in their actions. First, because power permits people to get their way more often, and induces people to be more positive in their outlook and pursue their goals with more vigor, when the powerful misbehave, they are held to be more responsible for that behavior. The higher degree of perceived agency would cause others to sanction the powerful more severely. Second, the researchers argued that higher-status, more powerful individuals were seen as acting more in their own self-interest and pursuing their own wellbeing, which would also lead to more severe sanctions because there would be less attribution of prosocial motivation. In two scenario studies, Fragale and her colleagues found that the higher the wrongdoers' status, the more severe the punishment observers wanted to mete out.[14]

Another mechanism: power leads to greater visibility and attention paid to the powerful. Therefore, misdeeds or failures of the powerful are more likely to draw greater notice and thus result in more social disapproval and sanctioning. For example, a study of the scandal of British members of Parliament overclaiming expenses— essentially fudging their expense reports—found that higher-status members were more likely to be targeted by the press and voters for inappropriate claims than their lower-status counterparts.[15]

The existing literature on punishment does not provide an unambiguous answer on the effects of social status on the severity of punishment, with some studies finding higher sanctions for high-power wrongdoers, and other research finding lower ones.[16] This ambiguity in results could arise for two reasons: either higher-status wrongdoers have more latitude and their behavior is evaluated less negatively, or lower-status wrongdoers evoke greater sympathy and receive some "credit" for their absence of power.[17]

Notwithstanding the greater visibility that accompanies power, attributions of greater potency and agency, and the fact that observers have less sympathy for the powerful, my sense is that power generally insulates people from suffering too greatly for the consequences of their actions, both for the reasons already adduced and the additional logic I outline next.

SOME EXAMPLES OF POWER AND WEALTH INSULATING WRONGDOERS

I argue that power and money insulate people from facing severe consequences for their actions, partly because people want to be close to money and power and are therefore willing either to forgive those who have them or avert their gaze from their possessors' misdeeds. Yet it is incumbent on me to provide at least some plausible evidence for this assertion about the insulating effects of power.

Although I know of no comprehensive listing of the wrongdoing of the powerful and the consequences they have (or haven't) faced, examples of the powerful escaping sanctions, particularly social sanctions, are plentiful.

Let's begin with ProPublica reporter and Pulitzer Prize–winning author Jesse Eisinger's book, *The Chickenshit Club*,[18] exploring why and how social changes have undermined the ability and motivation of prosecutors to go after white-collar criminals, with a particular focus on the absence of serious prosecutions emanating from the 2008 financial meltdown. Eisinger's argument is straightforward: many people who serve as prosecutors will subsequently go to work for the defense bar and therefore are already somewhat socially identified with their presumed adversaries. As a review of Eisinger's book argued:

> *Increasingly, the prosecutors and the defense attorneys on opposite sides of the table are the same people, just at different points in their careers. Conducting a criminal investigation of an executive isn't just risky; in addition to jeopardizing a future partnership at a prestigious law firm, perhaps most important, it incurs "social discomfort," especially for the well-mannered overachievers who now populate the Justice Department. No one wants to be a class traitor, especially when the members of one's class are such nice people.*[19]

This argument applies more generally, beyond the prosecutor–defense bar setting. People in power travel in similar circles, including social and charitable circles. They go to many of the same conferences and events, particularly with other powerful individuals from the same industry. They may serve on the same for-profit and nonprofit boards. These social connections, both direct and indirect, will invariably act to dampen not only any sense of outrage over the wrongdoing of similar others, but also the interest in sanctioning that wrongdoing. Thus, much to the surprise of outsiders, a get along–go along culture prevails and insulates the powerful from facing many, or any, consequences, almost regardless of what they have done.

As an example of this phenomenon: I am sitting in a nice office in the heart of Beverly Hills with a fundraising colleague from Stanford. I have been advised to look up the person we were going to visit, probably to ensure I was comfortable with the meeting. I learned from my online research that Gary Winnick, who had sold junk bonds at Drexel Burnham alongside Michael Milken, had founded Global Crossing in 1999 and raised nearly $20 billion to finance the laying of fiber optic cables all over the world. In 2002, Global Crossing declared bankruptcy. As the company was going under, Winnick sold $738 million in stock.[20] Later, he voluntarily contributed $55 million to a $324 million settlement with shareholders and former employees who had sued Global Crossing executives and directors for securities fraud. He also contributed $25 million to a $79 million settlement fund brokered by the Labor Department for former employees who had lost their pensions in the bankruptcy. In the end, Winnick avoided being criminally charged or sanctioned by the SEC (on a 3–2 vote that overruled the agency's staff).[21] So, unlike some of the people we will discuss in this chapter, he escaped suffering an actual legal loss in either criminal or civil cases.

If you do the math, Gary Winnick walked away with a lot of money—$738 million minus $80 million equals $658 million. He also owned one of the largest houses in Los Angeles. Winnick was and is an extremely generous benefactor to many, many charities. He received an honorary doctorate from his undergraduate institution, C. W. Post, *after* the Global Crossing debacle, probably because of his past—and possibly future—beneficence to that organization.

Winnick's office was decorated, as are many such offices, with pictures of him alongside notables—popes, presidents (from both political parties), mayors, members of Congress, dignitaries from multiple states, cities, and countries, and celebrities. Many of the pictures postdated the Global Crossing debacle. Winnick was living a life of power, privilege, and access—and, most importantly, one rich in important, notable, and powerful social connections.

Oh, I did mention he had worked at the same firm, Drexel Burnham, as Michael Milken? One day, watching an Oakland A's game on television, I saw and heard as a guest in the broadcast booth none other than Michael Milken, introduced by the play-by-play announcers as a philanthropist, which he most certainly is. A prostate cancer survivor, Milken has financed medical research. He has also funded a think tank, the Milken Institute, and numerous other charitable causes. But Milken is possibly most famous for inventing junk bond financing at Drexel Burnham, making a lot of people, many still on Wall Street, a lot of money. And in April 1990, "after four years of investigation and prosecution" and agreeing to "plead guilty to six charges of criminal violation of securities laws—technical violations, as opposed to the original 98-count indictment . . . and to pay a $600 million fine,"[22] Milken served twenty-two months in a minimum-security prison. He also paid $500 million to Drexel's private investors, who had lost money when the firm was liquidated. A 2017 profile of Milken describes him, I believe accurately, as "one of the most respected people on Wall Street." That article, by the financial journalist William Cohan, quotes someone who met him later in his life this way: "Mike Milken was kind of like Jim Jones [of Jonestown Massacre infamy] with a billion dollars, a PR man, and a fancy office."[23]

Success—money and power—takes care of many presumed sins, causing others to ignore, forget, or otherwise overlook or rationalize wrongdoing. Martha Stewart, a presumed billionaire and lifestyle doyenne, spent five months in prison after her 2004 conviction for obstruction of justice, making false statements, and conspiracy for lying to investigators in an insider trading case. Notwithstanding her criminal record, Stewart's brand has never been worth more. Her fashion and lifestyle advice remained in demand even after her sentencing, as the department store chains Macy's and J. C. Penney, who each thought she had an exclusive arrangement with them, used her brand and image to sell sheets, towels, and housewares.[24]

Jeffrey Epstein, the notorious sex offender, before being reinvestigated and taking his own life in a New York holding cell, was active in Florida and New York high society, even associating with a member of the British royal family. As one account noted, "In 2010, the year *after* [Epstein] got out of a Florida prison, Katie Couric and George Stephanopoulos dined at his Manhattan mansion with a British royal. The next year, Mr. Epstein was photographed at a 'billionaire's dinner' attended by tech titans like Jeff Bezos and Elon Musk."[25] A review of the book written by Julie K. Brown, the *Miami Herald* reporter who broke the story that finally took him down, noted that "less than a year before he died in a Manhattan jail cell . . . the self-proclaimed financier had many of the world's richest, smartest and most powerful men on speed dial." Many journalists "were wowed by access to him and blinded by the cadre of famous men who encircled him."[26] Epstein, after his first stint in jail, provided valuable—and highly compensated—services to Leon Black, a cofounder of Apollo, the private equity and investment management firm.

The phenomenon I'm describing applies to women as well as men. For instance, I was having dinner with a friend who is a senior HR executive and an occasional speaker in my power class. She told me that she was recently at a Silicon Valley social event where she met this amazingly charismatic, charming, powerful young woman. Would I like to meet her? Elizabeth Holmes, late of Theranos, was apparently raising money for her *next* venture. And notwithstanding the documentaries, articles, at the time, a pending criminal trial, and so forth associated with Theranos's collapse, Holmes was still well accepted in powerful social circles and apparently having some success in raising money for her second act.

I was not surprised that Elizabeth Holmes was moving so easily through such powerful circles and raising new money. Silicon Valley is full of such tales, in which wrongdoers are quickly forgiven and soon receive more financial backing for their next venture. Parker Conrad was a founder and the CEO of HR benefits software company Zenefits. He was forced to resign in February 2016, "amid allegations that the company had intentionally overestimated sales projections and was flouting laws by failing to obtain [insurance] broker licenses for . . . employees."[27] In 2017, Conrad founded Rippling, an employee-management software start-up. In August 2020, Rippling raised $145 million with a valuation of $1.35 billion, and Conrad had no trouble attracting money for the company at its inception, past legal and ethical issues notwithstanding.

In another example, Mike Cagney was ousted as chief executive from personal finance company Social Finance when the board found out he was romantically involved with an employee—and after he told them he was not involved in any extramarital workplace relationships. "Yet just months after Mr. Cagney departed SoFi, two venture capitalists who had been on the company's board and knew the many details of his actions invested $17 million in his new start-up . . . Since then, Mr. Cagney has raised another $41 million from others for the lending start-up . . . what happened in the past—even if it was in the immediate past—often becomes a marginal factor."[28]

Likewise, the story of Uber and its cofounder and former chief executive, Travis Kalanick, recounts how "the subterfuge—the lying, spying, bribery lawbreaking, and threats against reporters and competitors—worked . . . As long as Uber's private valuation climbed . . . even the more critical directors were willing to look past his misbehavior."[29]

To be clear, I am certainly *NOT* recommending that you commit crimes, engage in sexual predation, extract money while your company is going bankrupt, violate insurance or other regulations, or exaggerate the capabilities of your company or its products. But there's an extremely important lesson—for you and maybe for society—in these stories and the myriad similar tales: if you are successful, rich, powerful, and have many powerful and rich friends—a great social network—then that success and those connections will likely protect you (notice I used the word *likely*, not *inevitably*) from falling from power and grace, almost *regardless* of what you do. Simply put, once you are on top, at least in some sense of that term, what you did to get there will be forgotten, forgiven, or possibly both.

The fact that power insulates people from facing the full consequences of their behavior may help explain why powerful people misbehave in the first place. Some social psychologist colleagues have written about how power leads to disinhibition in people's behavior, lending the saying "Power corrupts" some empirical validity.[30] Power causes people to attend to rewards and gains rather than losses, increases their optimism, and leads them to engage in riskier behavior,[31] thus seemingly freeing people to do what they otherwise would not as they vigorously pursue their own goals with little regard for how their behavior affects others.

This chapter provides an additional plausible explanation for why this disinhibited, counter-normative behavior occurs more frequently on the part of the powerful. One reason that power may produce such violation of social norms and conventions is because power *insulates* people from the worst consequences of their actions, ensuring that they will not be called to account in the same way as the less powerful and wealthy. If power helps insulate people from the consequences of their behavior, it is scarcely surprising that the powerful will feel freer to do what they want.

I can anticipate what people are thinking—that all of these people eventually suffered consequences. As I write this, Elizabeth Holmes is facing sentencing for convictions on four counts of wire fraud. Parker Conrad was fired from Zenefits. Jeffrey Epstein died in a jail cell. Harvey Weinstein was convicted of rape, notwithstanding his power in Hollywood, and Woody Allen had movie projects canceled and distribution curtailed because of allegations of childhood sexual abuse.

Yet the negative consequences resulted from tremendous, and frequently rare, efforts. Epstein's downfall resulted in part because a local reporter—and there are ever fewer of them in the rapidly consolidating media ecosystem—decided to pursue the story of how a convicted felon was able to consort with the rich and famous even as he continued the predatory lifestyle that had caused him legal trouble. And notwithstanding that the *Miami Herald* supported Julie K. Brown's efforts, she nonetheless encountered numerous barriers as she pursued the story. Yes, maybe *New York Times* reporter Jodi Kantor will decide to look into a powerful wrongdoer's behavior, as she and colleague Megan Twohey did Harvey Weinstein's, resulting in a best-selling book and a Pulitzer Prize, and eventually Weinstein being jailed and his movie company shutting down. Note, however, that the people *finally* brought down engaged in particularly egregious behavior, and most did so over a very long time, until they had the bad luck to run up against people who cared about their behavior and were in a position to expose it. For most people most of the time, investigations will not be forthcoming and power will endure.

Our task is to understand the social psychology of *why* their power remains so stable, so you can avoid being surprised when power endures.

MOTIVATED COGNITION PROVIDES A MECHANISM FOR IGNORING MISBEHAVIOR

"People often believe that their thinking aims squarely at gaining an accurate impression of reality. Upon closer inspection, this assumption collapses."[32] The phenomenon of motivated cognition describes a ubiquitous, effortless, and pervasive process in "which the goals and needs of individuals steer their thinking towards desired conclusions."[33] Simply put, people see—and believe—what they want to. Many manifestations of motivated cognition operate to ensure that people in power retain their power. Here are a couple of the phenomenon's effects.

The Desire for Consistency and Its Effect on the Perception of Power Holders

The so-called cognitive consistency paradigm's core hypothesis is "that humans possess a deep-seated need for cognitive consistency, the frustration of which engenders distress."[34] The assumptions of cognitive consistency have had widespread take-up not only in psychology but also in organizational psychology, neuroscience, economics, sociology, and political science. Recently the core assumption of a need or drive for consistency has been critiqued, with the argument that the apparent effects of the drive for consistency can be better explained as something reflecting the updating of cognitive beliefs resulting from discrepant information rather than a fundamental human motive. For our purposes, the distinction is not particularly relevant, because in both instances, the empirical predictions are similar: cognitions tend toward consistency.

How this consistency effect plays out regarding power and its maintenance is straightforward. The cognition "Person X is powerful, rich, and successful" has implications for other beliefs about the person, such as they are moral, competent, intelligent, hardworking, and generally someone whose association would be desirable. Importantly, the attributions of someone's traits are more malleable than the attributions of power, wealth, and success, which have stronger anchors in facts. Jeff Bezos is unquestionably one of the richest people in the world. Donald Trump was elected president of the United States in 2016, and received the second-largest number of popular votes in US history in 2020. If consistency in cognition is to be attained, it is reasonably obvious that it is easier to believe traits about these or any other individuals that are congruent with their achievements than it is to deny the facts of their wealth or power.

The implication: once a person has achieved wealth, fame, status, or power—ideas that are conceptually distinct in theory but so frequently co-occur as to be not meaningfully distinguishable—people's consistency tendencies will create attributions that will reinforce beliefs in that person's power, potency, intelligence, and so forth, creating a self-reinforcing cycle.

Here's a research-based example of how consistency of beliefs operates. Berkeley business school professor Barry Staw noted the correlation between dimensions of work groups, organizations, and individuals and various performance outcomes. Staw argued, and then experimentally demonstrated, that although many scholars and others thought that the dimensions predicted performance, it could be that performance outcomes, once known, affected the attribution of group or organizational characteristics. He wrote:

> It is posited that organizational participants possess theories of performance just as do organizational researchers, and that respondents will use knowledge of performance as a cue by which they attribute characteristics to themselves, their work groups, and organizations. According to this attribution hypothesis, self-report data on organizational characteristics may actually represent the consequences rather than the determinants of performance.[35]

Staw's argument would apply not just to attributions of organizational performance, self-reports, or cross-sectional data. It also would apply to how people make inferences consistent with the observed facts about others. With respect to power, these inferences will almost invariably tend to reinforce perceptions that will make the person in power appear to deserve that power, thereby tending to ensure they remain powerful.

The Belief in a Just World and the Rationalization of Misbehavior

Most people want to believe that the world is a just and fair place and that folks mostly get what they deserve. As social psychologist Melvin Lerner noted when he developed the so-called just-world hypothesis, the idea of a just world provides people with a sense of predictability and control. Individuals love a feeling of certainty and influence over their environments. Believing in a just world means: follow the rules and you will prosper; break the rules—or laws—and you will suffer.

What some people do not recognize is that the reverse logic also operates. The belief that people get what they deserve implies that individuals who have suffered setbacks or reversals must have done something to deserve those things—a phenomenon that can slide into blaming the victim. Conversely, people who have prospered presumably deserve their good fortune—and this search for justifications for good (or bad) fortune extends to outcomes that occur purely by chance.

As another manifestation of cognitive consistency, just-world thinking operates to impute positive behaviors and traits to individuals who have succeeded in attaining power and wealth. Once those positive traits are associated with people, others will act accordingly toward them, seeking to become closer to them, help them out, sing their praises, and in numerous other ways help create the reality of power and status into the future.

MORAL RATIONALIZATION AS AN EXAMPLE OF MOTIVATED COGNITION

Three marketing scholars set out to solve a puzzle: how consumers could continue to support public figures, or companies and brands, that behaved immorally.[36] The problem for individuals is one of inconsistency. On the one hand, they may have deep and enduring attachments and preferences for the public figures or companies; on the other hand, most people view themselves as morally upstanding. The dilemma: How to resolve the potential inconsistency and tension between being a moral individual and supporting someone who has engaged in wrongdoing?

One process to resolve this inconsistency is moral rationalization. As described by the late social psychologist Albert Bandura and his colleagues, moral rationalization refers to strategies in which people redefine and reconceptualize the immoral behavior of other social actors by "(1) redefining harmful conduct, (2) minimizing a perpetrator's role in causing harm, (3) minimizing or distorting harm caused by a perpetrator, and (4) dehumanizing or blaming the victim."[37] Moral rationalization permits people to keep associating with wrongdoers by redefining the behavior as either not that bad or not really their fault.

Another process of resolving the inconsistency, introduced in the paper by the three marketing scholars, is called moral decoupling. In this process, observers admit that the people to whom they are attached and attracted have engaged in wrongdoing, but rationalize their continued attraction to and involvement with them by arguing that the immoral behavior is not relevant to the present context. Moral decoupling represents "a psychological separation process by which consumers [and others] selectively disassociate judgments of morality from judgments of performance."[38] So, for instance, golfer Tiger Woods's extramarital affairs are not relevant to his skill as a golfer, Bill Clinton's dalliance with Monica Lewinsky is not relevant to his ability to effectively manage the US economy, the various sexual peccadillos of corporate executives do not reflect their skills as business strategists or operational managers, and so forth. Because moral decoupling permits people to acknowledge the wrongdoing while arguing that it is not relevant to the judgments of performance that motivate continuing association with the wrongdoer, moral decoupling is cognitively easier to accomplish:

> We find that moral decoupling is easier to justify and feels less wrong than moral rationalization. Whereas moral rationalization requires people to condone otherwise immoral behavior and may threaten consumers' moral self-image, moral decoupling enables consumers to support a transgressor while simultaneously condemning the transgression. By disassociating performance from

morality one can support an immoral actor without being subject to self-reproach.[39]

My casual observation is that both moral rationalization and moral decoupling are frequently in play, but that moral decoupling is, indeed, the more frequent way in which people justify continuing to associate with others who have misbehaved. The fundamental point: people have many ways to cognitively revalue and redefine situations in order to keep fraternizing with powerful if problematic others when it is in their interests to do so, while maintaining their own sense of moral integrity.

THE DESIRE TO BE CLOSE TO (PERCEIVED) POWER AND SUCCESS AFFECTS PEOPLE'S RELATIONSHIPS WITH POWERFUL OTHERS

People are attracted to power and success; they seek it out and strive to be close to those who possess both. As a result, their prior relationships and judgments about others can and do change to accommodate their desire to be associated with and proximate to the success of the powerful. The implication: once someone acquires power, status, money—the trappings of success—people will alter their opinions and behaviors in ways that are (1) consistent with that power and (2) congruent with the desire to be close to powerful people. Here are a couple of examples.

Laura Esserman, breast cancer surgeon at the University of California, San Francisco, cofounder of a nonprofit driving change in medical care with an annual budget of around $80 million, and winner of awards too numerous to mention, was a former student who initially was reluctant to embrace many of the course principles. I wrote a case on her in late 2003, and after hearing the case discussion, she began to adjust her approach to incorporate the rules of power. Many people I interviewed for the case described

Esserman's boundless energy and flamboyance but also noted she polarized those who interacted with her. One person who was not a Laura fan was a very senior faculty member in oncology at UCSF, who had problems with Esserman's style. At the time of the case, they were often in conflict. Esserman explained:

> She's very different from me. She wears suits every day and is very orderly. She knows how the system works and how to ascend the ladder within the system . . . Once I came out of my car wearing a purple coat and a purple hat and she looked at me with absolute horror and said, "Oh my God, Laura, you look like you just stepped out of the Wizard of Oz." She was horrified by this kind of representation.[40]

Although the relationship between Esserman and this other individual was quite strained, in late 2015 it "magically" changed for the better. When Esserman was featured in a front-page story in the Science section of the *New York Times*, she received the following email from this same individual:

> I loved the NY Times article about you and just heard about the luminary award. You rock! I am so proud of all you have accomplished for women with breast cancer and for UCSF. You have managed to make things happen that I never thought were possible. Congratulations and here's to much more to come!

The aphorism that success has many parents but that failure is an orphan can be accurately restated as: when you are powerful and successful, you will have more friends than you ever knew you had; when you lose power, no one will know you.

To expand on that last point: because people seek to associate with others who have power, once someone loses their power, either through ouster, retirement, or voluntary resignation, the number of people who want to be close to them will diminish. Yale professor Jeffrey Sonnenfeld wrote an award-winning book, *The Hero's Farewell*, about CEOs ceding power graciously—or not—at the end of their careers.[41] He identified four types of corporate leaders: Monarchs who refuse to leave voluntarily, Generals who leave reluctantly and plan a comeback, Ambassadors who leave gracefully, and Governors who leave to pursue new and different challenges. The book, now more than thirty years old, argued that executive successions were frequently difficult because CEOs, who think of themselves as heroes, were often unwilling to surrender control of "their" firm. This phenomenon of not wanting to leave a position of power likely has grown more prevalent, when CEO salaries are far higher and the various perquisites of office substantially greater.

One motivation for people to hang on to positions of power, like CEO roles, is their recognition that once they are no longer in that role, the motivation for others to be associated with them diminishes dramatically, and therefore they can find themselves with much-reduced status—and personhood. A friend of mine, a former CEO of a large organization who then was in a very senior (but not top) role in yet another mammoth company in a different industry and now is running a start-up he founded, sent me this email: "I hope your experience has been different, but I have found that enduring friendships are hard to maintain as I get older. I truly value ours." I believe the issue this person confronted is not so much about aging; rather it reflects the consequences for interpersonal interactions arising from moving out of high-status/high-power roles into a position with less formal power and control over vast resources. And yes, many people are much less interested in someone at that point.

THOSE IN POWER GET TO WRITE— AND CREATE—HISTORY

People in power typically have access to resources, including financial and social capital—indeed, such capital may be the source of their power. They often use those resources to "create," in numerous ways, a history that whitewashes past misdeeds or reinterprets them in ways favorable to them. By writing their own story, the powerful can highlight those aspects of their careers that create a favorable image while ignoring incidents that would portray them in a less-than-desirable light. If they succeed in getting their stories widely promulgated, these become the "official" account of their life—which can further perpetuate their power.

Because writing one's own history is so important to creating and perpetuating power, numerous people have done so. Table 7-1 presents a brief, partial list of the many leaders who have told their own tales.

TABLE 7-1	A (VERY) PARTIAL LIST OF BUSINESS AUTOBIOGRAPHERS
Author	**Company**
Jack Welch	General Electric
Lee Iacocca	Chrysler
Henry Ford	Ford Motors
Alfred P. Sloan	General Motors
Andrew Grove	Intel
Marc Benioff	Salesforce
Thomas J. Watson Jr.	IBM
Michael Dell	Dell Computer
Michael Eisner	Disney
Robert Iger	Disney
Phil Knight	Nike
Mary Kay Ash	Mary Kay Cosmetics
Ray Kroc	McDonald's
David Packard	Hewlett-Packard

Howard Schultz	Starbucks
Sam Walton	Walmart
Reid Hoffman	LinkedIn
Kim Scott	Dropbox
John Mackey	Whole Foods
Tony Hsieh	Zappos
Sir Richard Branson	Virgin Records, Airlines, and others
Satya Nadella	Microsoft
Carly Fiorina	Hewlett-Packard
Michael Bloomberg	Bloomberg
Yvon Chouinard	Patagonia
Stephen Schwarzman	Blackstone
Peter Thiel	PayPal and others
David Novak	YUM! Brands
Martha Stewart	Martha Stewart Living Omnimedia
Jason Fried	Basecamp
Bernie Marcus and Arthur Blank	Home Depot
Andrew Yang	Manhattan Prep (test preparation) and political candidate
Ken Langone	Venture capitalist, instrumental in financing Home Depot
Meg Whitman	eBay

In chapter four, I noted how many business leaders and political figures, possibly now more than ever, write books that burnish their image. That this is only a partial list of business autobiographies shows just how extensive this activity has been.

The ability to create a narrative and then tell it repeatedly until it becomes seen as truth helps people retain their power. The fact is that venture capitalists, other investors, and even employees and customers love a nice founding myth about an enterprise, which typically elevates the role of one entrepreneur and writes their colleagues out of the picture. As long as the story "sells," inspires, and has some element of truth, observers won't care about its full veracity. They are interested in the vision, in the narrative, in creating a tale useful for attracting investment, customers, and employees, not something historically accurate. Therefore, the ability to get one's story out early, often, and convincingly creates a reality that can then perpetuate a person's power, regardless of any inconvenient disconfirming facts.

The case of Jack Dorsey illustrates the dynamics of this process. As nicely described by technology reporter Nick Bilton,[42] Dorsey contributed to the founding of Twitter but did not conceive the idea behind it, nor was he there when its predecessor company, Odeo, a maker of podcasts, was created by Evan Williams. Dorsey did become chief executive of Twitter, but he was not a great manager and was forced out of the company. What happened next was consistent with the idea of this chapter that success, or the illusion of success, can make all things right—and reconstruct an image:

> After he was stripped of his power at Twitter, Dorsey went on a media campaign to promote the idea that he and Williams had switched roles. He also began telling a more elaborate story about the founding of Twitter. In dozens of interviews, Dorsey completely erased Glass [Noah Glass, the originator of the idea] from any involvement in the genesis of the company. He changed his biography on Twitter to "inventor"; before long, he started to exclude Williams and Stone too. At an event, Dorsey complained to Barbara Walters that he had founded Twitter, a point she raised the next day on "The View" . . . Dorsey told the Los Angeles

*Times that "Twitter had been my life's work in many senses." He
also failed to credit Glass for the company's unusual name . . .
Dorsey's story evolved over the years . . . Dorsey began cast-
ing himself in the image of Steve Jobs . . . adopting a singular
uniform: a white buttoned-up Dior shirt, bluejeans, and a black
blazer . . . In Silicon Valley, most companies have their own Twitter story: a co-founder, always a friend, and often the person with
the big idea behind the company, who is pushed out by another,
hungrier co-founder. As one former Twitter employee has said,
"The greatest product Jack Dorsey ever made was Jack Dorsey."*[43]

In the end, the reality of Jack Dorsey, who is now worth billions
of dollars, becomes the story that was made up. At this point, no
one, other than maybe some journalists and professors, really cares
about the actual origins of Twitter or Jack Dorsey's makeover. Power
gets to write history, and in so doing, helps perpetuate the power
itself, and many of the foundations on which it was built.

EVERYTHING'S FOR SALE— EVEN RESPECTABILITY

Madonna, the Queen of Pop, said it best: "We are living in a material world." In such a world, it is more than Madonna's companionship (as in the song) that is for sale—almost everything is. Or,
put another way, much of life, including social life, is more transactional than we like to think.

Power is often associated with wealth, but even when it is not,
power and its associated status and prestige can be used to generate financial resources. Those resources can then be deployed as
gifts to prestigious, high-status nonprofit organizations to "purchase" social status and legitimacy. People's names on or associated
with legitimate, high-status institutions helps confer respectabil-
ity on the donors. Not surprisingly, then, for people with wealth,

donations with their names attached are an oft-used strategy to provide insurance that they will be seen in a favorable light and their bad behavior overlooked or forgotten.

To quote a *New Yorker* article about how charity can be used to cloak wrongdoing or compensate for it, using Bill Cosby and Harvey Weinstein as examples:

> One view is that philanthropy can operate as a kind of penance mechanism. The individual who recognizes that he has done wrong attempts to make good in equal measure, to place a thumb on the scale of karma . . . We just recognized the annual awarding of an international peace prize created by a man [Nobel] who grew rich from the sales of dynamite and the attendant war munitions. Many of the great name-brand foundations were created in honor of individuals whose personal character or wealth was connected to deeply morally compromising actions.[44]

Consider the use of charitable donations by some of the people already mentioned in this chapter to improve their image. Michael Milken, according to his spokesman, has donated more than $1 billion to medical research, education, and other causes. In 2014, "George Washington University renamed its School of Public Health the Milken Institute School of Public Health."[45] Martha Stewart, winner of WebMD's 2014 People's Choice award, "with a $5 million donation . . . opened the Martha Stewart Center for Living at Mount Sinai Hospital in New York," filling a need for quality healthcare for seniors.[46] Elizabeth Holmes held a fundraiser in Palo Alto for Hillary Clinton's 2016 campaign. The Winnicks have been important donors to Mrs. Winnick's alma mater, Syracuse University, and Mr. Winnick's, Long Island University. The Winnicks also donated naming grants to the Winnick Children's Zoo in Los Angeles, Winnick Hillel House at Syracuse University, the Winnick Board Room at the Museum of Modern Art in New York City, and the Winnick International Conference Center of the Simon Wiesenthal Center in Jerusalem, among a long list of charitable institutions.[47]

SOME IMPLICATIONS

Vince Lombardi, legendary coach of the Green Bay Packers, is credited with the saying, "Winning isn't everything, it's the only thing," although football coach Henry "Red" Sanders of UCLA may have said it first.[48] Lombardi, Sanders, and others who have said the same thing since were making the case that winning is very important. There is another way to interpret this adage, however. It is that winning—in this case, reaching a position of great power—becomes "the only thing" because winning, with the power, status, and wealth it brings, renders much else unimportant or irrelevant.

This is not to say that the powerful do not fall from grace. But their ability to maintain association with high-status institutions, and to ensure that their story is effectively told in ways that burnish their reputations—and the fact that power, because of how consistency effects operate, causes people to find ways to justify and rationalize and honor those in power—can make power self-perpetuating.

Power is scarcely the only social domain where self-perpetuating, self-confirming forces are at play; the self-fulfilling prophecy concept is a useful way of understanding many phenomena. But the fact that power does provide some degree of insulation for the powerful has important implications for those who seek to take down the powerful, and also for people thinking about how and *if* to build their power. Simply put, once you are in power, you are likely to remain there because of all of the processes I have described in this chapter. And much of what you have done to achieve power will indeed be forgiven or forgotten as people construct stories based on the twin desires for consistency and to be close to those in power.

CODA
Staying on the Path to Power

As my colleague Bob Sutton and I noted in *The Knowing-Doing Gap*,[1] knowledge may be helpful, but knowledge not turned into action is of little to no value. That fact is also true about power: knowing the rules of power provides advantage only to the extent people turn that knowledge into action, and do so frequently. Furthermore, acting on knowledge facilitates learning from the experience that action provides, and much like any practice, action helps make that knowledge endure as it becomes part of people's regular behaviors. Therefore, I end the book with some advice on how to turn knowledge about the rules of power into actions that can create a path to power.

The first word of advice: learn about power, and then relearn what you have learned again and again, because the material, while easy to understand, is apparently more difficult to implement than it should be.

Some years ago, I met Rajiv Pant, then the chief technology officer for the *New York Times*. Rajiv went on to work for Arianna Huffington at Thrive, then was chief product and technology officer at the *Wall Street Journal*. He recently joined Hearst Corporation. He initially reached out to me through email.

"How did you find me," I inquired.

"Through your book, *Power*,"[2] was his reply.

And how did Pant come to see the book? He had been in information technology at Condé Nast Publications, where he had lost a political battle to a rival who had completely outmaneuvered him. Pant knew he needed to leave the company to regain his career momentum. He decided to graciously admit defeat and leave on as good of terms as possible with the person who had bested him. Going to his rival—now boss's—office to have a final conversation, he noticed the spine of my book on the bookshelf. He decided to purchase and read it. As he told me, he now knew what had happened to him.

Determined not to have this happen again, Pant bought three versions of *Power*: an audio version, a Kindle version, and a hard copy. Why three versions of the same content? Because, as he said to me, "What you are asking us to do is unnatural—it goes against how we were raised and what we have been taught in school. What you are teaching is also inconsistent with what we are regularly told in the ubiquitous—and mostly useless—leadership trainings and books that mostly describe how people want the social world to be, rather than the empirical regularities that explain what actually works to build power and get things done." As implied by the writing of Machiavelli, and by understanding the social science of human behavior, as one person perceptively noted to me, "Leadership is not a moral pursuit." It is above all about the pragmatics of making things happen.

Doing things that are unnatural, and in some sense counter to conventional wisdom, requires reminders and constant vigilance. That's because, by definition, unnatural behaviors do not come naturally, and are therefore difficult to implement and demand conscious thought and attention.

Precisely. Pant's analysis has some important implications. The world is hierarchical, with fewer positions at the top than at the bottom, whether you are talking about professional sports, universities, companies, political organizations, or school districts. In a hierarchical world with competition for advancement, the ability to do power becomes increasingly important as your career advances, because other differentiators among people, such as intelligence or technical skills, become more and more equal as individuals rise through the ranks. At a certain level, everybody is smart and has approximately the same technical knowledge. If doing power were easy or natural, it would not be such an important differentiating factor in people's ability to achieve higher positions or their objectives. If almost everyone could easily and readily implement the rules of power, doing so would provide an advantage to almost no one.

Because the lessons and principles of this book do not come naturally to many, and are not automatic or easy to do, the implication is obvious. You need to get help in thinking through and applying these seven rules in your life. Here are some ideas about how to do that.

Get a Personal Coach

I keep a list of people who have worked with my online and on-campus classes. These are people who understand the ideas and have excellent coaching skills. I offer this list to people who ask me about finding executive coaching resources. Of course, people are free to find their own executive coach—I'm not getting any commissions from making recommendations. But choose them carefully. Pick someone you can connect with and learn from, and most importantly, who will not just offer you tea and sympathy, but also have you think about your mistakes, so you don't make them again. Here's an example of what I consider to be bad coaching advice.

At a lunch, I was sitting across from an extremely talented MIT-trained engineer who cofounded a company that was sold to Google, although she was forced out of the firm prior to the sale by her cofounder. The precipitating event of her departure was the hiring of a strongly talented, apparently value-creating marketing executive who, at the last minute before accepting the offer, told her cofounder that he could not work with and particularly for a woman.

I looked at that woman and asked what she did. She said she left for the good of the company, something that was emotionally hard for her to do. She subsequently told this incident to her personal coach, who replied by accusing the marketing executive of being a sexist pig and her cofounder of extreme disloyalty.

"What else did the coach say?" I asked. "Nothing," was her reply—the coach provided a sympathetic ear and emotional support in the context of a traumatic event.

My response was immediate: "Fire your coach." Why? Because while the coach's statements about the cofounder and the marketing executive were undoubtedly true, they were completely unhelpful in teaching my lunch partner how she was complicit in her own disempowerment.

I asked, "Did you actually know for a fact that this marketing executive said that he would not work for or with you?" My lunch partner said no, she had not explored the possibility that her cofounder had made the story up as a way of getting her out of the company or that, faced with not getting the job, the marketing person would not change his mind. She couldn't believe her cofounder would make up this story to get her out of the organization.

I continued: "What would your cofounder have done had the tables been turned, and he had to leave for the company to be able to recruit some important executive talent?" He probably would not have left, she told me.

My expression conveyed my thought: *Why were you so willing to sacrifice your role when you knew, or at least strongly suspected, that he would not do the same for you, and moreover, you did not have firsthand knowledge of the situation that forced you out of the company you had cofounded and where you added so much value?*

Aghast, she looked at me, and complained that I was "blaming the victim." I responded that "blaming" was not a term that I would use, but that while the behavior she had confronted was reprehensible, she could not control the perpetrators, nor people that she might encounter in the future with similarly awful viewpoints and actions. The hard lesson: the only individual whose behavior she had reasonably complete control of was, of course, her own. Therefore, she needed to figure out what to do differently.

I continued: "This type of situation will, unfortunately, possibly arise again. You don't need a coach to provide you sympathy. You need a coach who will prepare you, psychologically and strategically, to deal with such an occurrence more effectively in the future—at a minimum by standing your ground."

The moral of the story: find a coach who will nicely, constructively, but firmly push you outside of your comfort zone, and get you to think hard about *your* choices and *your* actions—the only things over which you have control—so you can prevail in power struggles. Yes, the world can be cruel and unfair. As I tell my students, if you are ever done in, it is likely to be by those closest to you. They are the ones who have both the motive and the opportunity, as in the case of my lunch companion's start-up and cofounder. Who betrays Julius Caesar in the Shakespeare play? Brutus, "Caesar's friend and a man of honour."[3] Be prepared, so when bad, unfair things happen, you are not surprised and can respond effectively, strategically, and as unemotionally as possible.

Set Up a Personal Board of Directors

What does a good, well-functioning board do for a company? It provides fresh perspectives, different information, and, in the best of cases, holds the leadership team responsible for results. This may be precisely what you need: a set of people (maybe three or four) who don't need to meet as a group, who work in different industries and occupations and thus are in no way structurally or otherwise competitive with you. Their job is to hold you accountable for the objectives you set for yourself, to offer you different information, perspectives, and contacts than you can access on your own, and to provide you an element of personal coaching. People are frequently willing to do this because, as we explored with the topic of asking for help in chapter two, people love to be helpful and offer advice and assistance.

Set Up a "Power Posse" or Organize "Power Lunches"

In the last few years, several groups of women from my class have spontaneously decided to get together regularly during the quarter they are taking the class and afterward, sometimes even after they have graduated. The underlying principle behind this activity is to brainstorm with similarly situated others who are not competing with you about ways to take general ideas—which is what this book and my class are mostly about—and translate them into specific actions in specific situations. Research shows that brainstorming with others is a good way of getting new ideas and learning.[4] That is also true for brainstorming about how to do power more effectively. The idea of a weekly lunch (or dinner) is to maintain momentum, obtain the benefits of social facilitation—the idea that people perform better and are more motivated in the presence of others[5]—build social support, and have a pleasant social interaction even as you are thinking through tough issues about navigating organizational politics.

Tamar Nisbett, a Black woman from my class now working in finance, described how, in 2020, what came to be called the Power Posse began. She and some classmates tried some of the things from the class, and they worked. A student from the prior year described how she had started Power Lunches. Nisbett reached out to her

about what she did and how it worked. Tamar and another classmate, Marta Milkowska, then invited six other women to join them:

> So that we'd have a group of eight, most of whom had taken the
> class already, because we were doing it for the first time. We
> decided to do eight weeks, and take our favorite chapter from the
> book, or the ones we found the most challenging, and focus on
> those, so each week had a theme. We would, as a group of women,
> meet at lunch on Mondays, talk about the themes, and mention if
> we needed help with anything. I think that was really nice because
> it allowed this group of amazing women to ask for help every sin-
> gle week, which is not something I think we had been used to. And
> it also gave us a chance to report on our progress, to be encouraged
> by other people who knew exactly what we were doing. It contin-
> ued in the spring. Marta and I are currently working on a pilot in
> the fall with three groups of MBAs, three groups of alumni GSB
> [Stanford Graduate School of Business] women, and three groups
> of non-GSB MBA women. We're currently building out a web-
> site and an education platform so that people can go through the
> learning on their own. It was so powerful for us, we want other
> women to have the opportunity to have that same sort of group
> where there is no fear in asking for help.

You do not have to be an MBA, or at Stanford, to do precisely
what these women have done. You don't even have to be a woman,
or live in the US. The power of being able to discuss ideas, particularly difficult or challenging ideas, with others, and the benefits
of being able to share your experiences with and ask for help from
them, is completely generalizable.

Make Lists

List what you want to do, what you want to learn, who you need
to meet. Keith Ferrazzi, marketing expert, speaker, and best-selling

author, told my class that "all my life I've made lists of things I wanted to accomplish." Lists provide you with specific goals of what you want to achieve and the steps required. Long-standing research on the topic reports that setting goals, particularly specific and ambitious objectives, positively affects your likelihood of achieving them and your overall level of performance.[6]

If doing power doesn't come naturally to you, practice. A friend who is a former golf pro told me that the golf swing is not a natural motion, so obtaining and keeping a good swing requires practice. Build what some people call your "power muscles" the same way you would build any other muscle: through practice and use. It is not that difficult. Figure out who can be helpful to you and reach out to them, practicing the idea of Rule 5. Build a powerful brand—Rule 4—by developing a concise statement of who you are and why you are uniquely qualified to be doing what you're doing. Act and speak with power—Rule 3—by understanding and then implementing the ideas of how to convey power through your facial expressions, body language, and words. Get out of your own way—Rule 1—by not holding yourself back and unnecessarily worrying about what everyone else is thinking about you. And break the rules—Rule 2—to surprise others by being resourceful in your power strategies and tactics. As you learn through thoughtful, reflective practice, you will see the results of turning this power knowledge into action in a relatively short time.

Keep the principles and information from this book in your mind. Reread it. Listen to an audio version during your commute. Discuss it with friends. Learn even more about the subject matter of power. Google makes the world's research available (at least in the form of article abstracts) via Google Scholar (scholar.google.com). Instead of speculating about things such as whether being agreeable is an advantage or disadvantage in climbing the corporate ladder and earning more money, or relying on anecdotes—or worse yet, some internet discussion, or the fictionalized account of some business leader's career as told in their self-enhancing, often ghost-written autobiographies—look things up. Learn the truth. Knowledge is power, and in today's world, it is literally at your fingertips. Access that knowledge—and then use it.

In a situation where you need to do things that are unnatural and maybe even uncomfortable, get people to help you. And continue doing things for yourself that will keep important ideas in your head even as you hold yourself accountable for, to paraphrase Stanford business school's motto, "changing lives, changing organizations, and changing the world."

I would wish you good luck in this endeavor—on your path to power. But luck has little to do with it. Instead, I wish you all the power that you seek.

ACKNOWLEDGMENTS

Writing a book, even one that is sole-authored, is very much a collective effort. Throughout my career I have been blessed, a word I use intentionally, with amazingly fabulous colleagues with whom I have done research and, independent of any joint work, who have provided insights and inspiration and the constructive critiques and challenges that have made my writing and thinking better. My life, and my work, has been so enriched by all of them. My teaching and research on power is specifically indebted to Cameron Anderson, Peter Belmi, Dana Carney, Robert Cialdini, Deborah Gruenfeld, the late Huseyin Leblebici, William Moore, Charles A. O'Reilly, the late Gerald Salancik, and Bob Sutton.

I owe a huge thanks to the many people who shared their stories with me over the years, and a particular shout-out to the people who permitted me to use their names. Some of them were students in my classes, some of them were protagonists in cases I wrote, and all of them have earned my undying gratitude. Thanks to Rukaiyah Adams, Jason Calacanis, Nuria Chinchilla, Alison Davis-Blake, Laura Esserman, Sadiq Gillani, the late John Jacobs, Tadia James, Jon Levy, Deb Liu, Gary Loveman, Rajiv Pant, Jeffrey Sonnenfeld, Christina Troitino, Ross Walker, and Tristan Walker.

I have been able to try out material and thoughts about power and influence on executive audiences because of the invitations of Stanford colleagues Bill Barnett, Peter DeMarzo, Buck Gee, Wes

Hom, Brian Lowery, Charles O'Reilly, Baba Shiv, and Larissa Tiedens, among others. For many years I taught my material on power in a program at IESE designed and directed by my friend and colleague Fabrizio Ferraro. My time with Fabrizio and his significant other, Laura, is a wonderful gift. I was able to visit IESE because the dean when I first visited, Jordi Canals, and then his successor, Franz Heukamp, made me and Kathleen welcome in ways too numerous to mention. I treasure my visits to IESE, and also to Bocconi, where Marco Tortoriello and I ran a short version of the Getting Things Done program.

Some years ago, I decided to increase the amount of feedback and executive coaching offered as part of my Paths to Power class. The six coaches who have worked with me in the class provided enormous value to the students and insights and suggestions that have helped me make the class and my teaching experience immeasurably better and more pleasurable. Thanks to Lauren Capitani, Jonathan Daves, Inbal Demri, Raquel Gonzalez Dalmau, Phillip Mohabir, and Kevin Williams—and to Michael Wenderoth, who has worked with the online version of the course from the beginning.

I never for a nanosecond take the fabulous support of the Graduate School of Business at Stanford for granted, including the support to hire these wonderful coaches and various people who have helped with my research. I treasure the time provided for me to do my writing and course development. I work at the best business school in the world. My now more than forty years here have been so special.

My agent, Christy Fletcher, whom I have worked with for many years, provided as always tremendously useful guidance, advice, support, and help with placing the book appropriately. My editor, Matt Holt at BenBella Books, and his colleagues have been a joy to work with as they have helped me make this book better and supported its marketing and distribution.

And, of course, there was always Kathleen, whom I met at a party in the Green Room of the War Memorial Opera House in San

Francisco on January 19, 1985, and married on July 23, 1986. As she would say, no algorithm would have matched us.

On August 27, 2020, at 1 PM, the phone rang in our home and on the other end was someone from our dentist's office telling me that Kathleen had limped into her appointment. Kathleen did not believe, given her healthy lifestyle and the fact that she looked decades younger than she was, that anything could be wrong, so she had not gone to a hospital but had somehow managed to drive to the dentist. The person on the line said that, weak on her right side, they did not think she should drive home. Thus began an odyssey that ended tragically.

Kathleen had suffered a stroke, which a neurologist said was very small but located in a very, very bad place in her brain. Her face, voice, ability to swallow, and persona, including her ability to make her wishes known (otherwise known as giving orders), were unaffected. But her right arm and leg were very severely weakened, to the point that by the time the full effects of the stroke kicked in, she could not transfer herself, bathe herself, or care for herself. In the ensuing year, we had 24-7 live-in care, help from numerous physical and occupational therapists, personal trainers, and massage therapists to help her regain her independence and reduce her pain, and the unending flowers and food sent by our many friends whose good wishes and prayers were so lovely and important.

In the beginning, in the midst of the COVID pandemic, I could not visit Kathleen until she arrived a few days later to the acute rehabilitation facility at California Pacific Medical Center—Davies Campus in San Francisco. When I saw her for the first time and gazed at her beautiful smile, I told her that we had met at a dance now more than thirty-five years ago, and that my hope and wish was to have her recover sufficiently so that we could have one more, one last, dance. I also told her that if she wanted to leave (as in this earth), I would not stand in her way.

Approximately one year later, on September 10, 2021, confronted with insufficient recovery that left her independence still compromised, in the house in San Francisco where she lived when I first met her, Kathleen engineered the process that ended her life. She died on September 11, ironically in the same hospital where she had begun her rehabilitation.

It is impossible for me to convey how sad, how devastated, I am as I write these words. Kathleen Frances Fowler was my family, my best friend, my lover, my spouse. My world revolved around her. This book, like many that have come before, is dedicated to her, to what she meant to me, and to the amazing love she gave to me over our many years together. She once told me that she believed we were together in prior lives and will be again in the future. I hope she is right. Because we never had that one last dance. I will love her forever.

ENDNOTES

IN THE BEGINNING

1. Jeffrey Pfeffer, *Power in Organizations*, Marshfield, MA: Pitman, 1981; Jeffrey Pfeffer, *Managing with Power: Politics and Influence in Organizations*, Boston: Harvard Business School Press, 1992; Jeffrey Pfeffer, *Power: Why Some People Have It—and Others Don't*, New York: Harper Business, 2010.
2. Jeffrey Pfeffer, *Leadership BS: Fixing Workplace and Careers One Truth at a Time*, New York: Harper Business, 2015.
3. George A. Miller (1956), "The Magical Number Seven, Plus or Minus Two: Some Limits on Our Capacity for Processing Information," *Psychological Review, 63* (2), 81–97; quote is from p. 81.
4. T. L. Saaty and M. S. Ozdemir (2003), "Why the Magic Number Seven Plus or Minus Two," *Mathematical and Computer Modelling, 38* (3–4), 233–244; quote is from p. 233.
5. Michael Marmot, *The Status Syndrome: How Social Standing Affects Our Health and Longevity*, New York: Times Books, 2004.
6. Y. Kifer, D. Heller, W. Q. E. Perunovic, and A. D. Galinsky (2003), "The Good Life of the Powerful: The Experience of Power and Authenticity Enhances Subjective Well-Being," *Psychological Science, 24* (3), 280–288.
7. Moses Naim, *The End of Power: From Boardrooms to Battlefields and Churches to States, Why Being in Charge Isn't What It Used to Be*, New York: Basic Books, 2014.
8. Steven Poole, "Why Would Mark Zuckerberg Recommend the End of Power?" *The Guardian*, January 8, 2015.

9. Kara Swisher, "Zuckerberg's Free Speech Bubble," *New York Times*, June 3, 2020. https://nyti.ms/2XsVM9a.

10. David Dayen, "The New Economic Concentration: The Competition That Justifies Capitalism Is Being Destroyed—by Capitalists," *American Prospect*, January 16, 2019. https://prospect.org/power/new -economic-concentration/.

11. Jeremy Heimans and Henry Timms, *New Power: How Power Works in Our Hyperconnected World—and How to Make It Work for You*, New York: Doubleday, 2018.

12. Ben Smith, "News Sites Risk Wrath of Autocrats," *New York Times*, July 13, 2020.

13. "Global Democracy Has Another Bad Year," *The Economist*, January 22, 2020. https://www.economist.com/graphic-detail/2020/01/22/global -democracy-has-another-bad-year.

14. Cato Institute, *The Human Freedom Index 2020*. https://www.cato.org /human-freedom-index-new.

15. Glenn Kessler, Salvador Rizzo, and Meg Kelly, *Donald Trump and His Assault on Truth: The President's Falsehoods, Misleading Claims and Flat-Out Lies*, New York: Scribner, 2020.

16. Frank Dikotter, *How to Be a Dictator: The Cult of Personality in the Twentieth Century*, New York: Bloomsbury, 2019.

17. J. M. Fenster, *Cheaters Always Win: The Story of America*, New York: Twelve, 2019.

18. Deborah L. Rhode, *Cheating: Ethics in Everyday Life*, New York: Oxford University Press, 2018.

19. Matthew Hutson, "Life Isn't Fair," *The Atlantic*, June 2016. https://www .theatlantic.com/magazine/archive/2016/06/life-isnt-fair/480741/.

20. Murray Edelman, *The Symbolic Uses of Politics*, Urbana: University of Illinois Press, 1964.

INTRODUCTION

1. Martin J. Smith, "Rukaiyah Adams, MBA '08, Chief Investment Officer, Meyer Memorial Trust," Stanford Graduate School of Business, May 9, 2019. https://gsb.stanford.edu/programs/mba/alumni -community/voices/rukaiyah-adams.

2. Sarah Lyons-Padilla, Hazel Rose Markus, Ashby Monk, Sid Radhakrishna, Radhika Shah, Norris A. "Daryn" Dodson IV, and Jennifer L. Eberhardt, "Race Influences Professional Investors' Financial

Judgments," *Proceedings of the National Academy of Sciences*, 116 (35), 17225–17230. https://www.pnas.org/cgi/doi/10.1073/pnas.1822052116.

3. *Los Angeles Times*, "John Jacobs; Columnist, Award-Winning Author," May 25, 2000. https://www.latimes.com/archives/la-xpm-2000-may -25-me-33886-story.html.

4. Tim Reiterman and John Jacobs, *Raven: The Untold Story of the Rev. Jim Jones and His People*, New York: E. P. Dutton, 1985.

5. Mark A. Whatley, Matthew Webster, Richard H. Smith, and Adele Rhodes (1999), "The Effect of a Favor on Public and Private Compliance: How Internalized Is the Norm of Reciprocity?" *Basic and Applied Social Psychology*, 21 (3), 251–259.

6. Reiterman and Jacobs, *Raven*, particularly chapter twenty-eight, "San Francisco in Thrall."

7. Charles A. O'Reilly and Jennifer A. Chatman (2020), "Transformational Leader or Narcissist? How Grandiose Narcissists Can Create and Destroy Organizations and Institutions," *California Management Review*, 62 (3), 5–27.

8. Bella M. DePaulo, Deborah A. Kashy, Susan E. Kirkendol, Melissa M. Wyer, and Jennifer A. Epstein (1996), "Lying in Everyday Life," *Journal of Personality and Social Psychology*, 70 (5), 979–995.

9. Elizabeth Prior Jonson, Linda McGuire, and Brian Cooper (2016), "Does Teaching Ethics Do Any Good?" *Education + Training*, 58 (4), 439–454.

10. Aditya Simha, Josh P. Armstrong, and Joseph F. Albert (2012), "Attitudes and Behaviors of Academic Dishonesty and Cheating—Do Ethics Education and Ethics Training Affect Either Attitudes or Behaviors?" *Journal of Business Ethics Education*, 9, 129–144.

11. James Weber (1990), "Measuring the Impact of Teaching Ethics to Future Managers: A Review, Assessment, and Recommendations," *Journal of Business Ethics*, 9, 183–190.

12. Christian Hauser (2020), "From Preaching to Behavior Change: Fostering Ethics and Compliance Learning in the Workplace," *Journal of Business Ethics*, 162, 835–855; quote is from p. 836.

13. Frank Martela (2015), "Fallible Inquiry with Ethical Ends-in-View: A Pragmatist Philosophy of Science for Organizational Research," *Organization Studies*, 36 (4), 537–563.

14. Columbia 250, "Robert Moses," accessed September 16, 2021. https://c250.columbia.edu/c250_celebrates/remarkable_columbians/robert _moses.html.

15. Yona Kifer, Daniel Heller, Wei Qi, Elaine Perunovic, and Adam D. Galinsky (2013), "The Good Life of the Powerful: The Experience of Power and Authenticity Enhances Subjective Well-Being," *Psychological Science, 24* (3), 280–288.
16. Kifer et al., "The Good Life of the Powerful," p. 283.
17. Gerlad R. Ferris, Pamela L. Perrewe, B. Parker Ellen III, Charn P. Mcallister, and Darren C. Treadway, *Political Skill at Work*, Boston: Nicholas Brealey Publishing, 2020; quote is from p. 15.
18. Ferris et al., *Political Skill at Work*, p. 27.
19. Samuel Y. Todd, Kenneth J. Harris, Ranida B. Harris, and Anthony R. Wheeler (2009), "Career Success Implications of Political Skill," *Journal of Social Psychology, 149* (3), 179–204.
20. Gerhard Blickle, Katharina Oerder, and James K. Summers (2010), "The Impact of Political Skill on Career Success of Employees' Representatives," *Journal of Vocational Behavior, 77* (3), 383–390.
21. Kathleen K. Ahearn, Gerald R. Ferris, Wayne A. Hochwarter, Caesar Douglas, and Anthony Ammeter (2004), "Leader Political Skill and Team Performance," *Journal of Management, 30* (3), 309–327.
22. Timothy P. Munyon, James K. Summers, Katina M. Thompson, and Gerald R. Ferris (2013), "Political Skill and Work Outcomes: A Theoretical Extension, Meta-Analytic Investigation, and Agenda for the Future," *Personnel Psychology, 68*, 143–184.
23. Li-Qun Wei, Flora F. T. Chiang, and Long-Zeng Wu (2010), "Developing and Utilizing Network Resources: Roles of Political Skill," *Journal of Management Studies, 49* (2), 381–402.
24. Kenneth J. Harris, K. Michel Kacmer, Suzanne Zivnuska, and Jason D. Shaw (2007), "The Impact of Political Skill on Impression Management Effectiveness," *Journal of Applied Psychology, 92* (1), 278–285.
25. Darren C. Treadway, Gerald R. Ferris, Allison B. Duke, Garry L. Adams, and Jason B. Thatcher (2007), "The Moderating Role of Subordinate Political Skill on Supervisors' Impressions of Subordinate Ingratiation and Ratings of Subordinate Interpersonal Facilitation," *Journal of Applied Psychology, 92* (3), 848–855.
26. Li-Qun Wei, Jun Liu, Yuan-Yi Chen, and Long-Zeng Wu (2010), "Political Skill, Supervisor-Subordinate *Guanxi* and Career Prospects in Chinese Firms," *Journal of Management Studies, 47* (3), 437–454.
27. Pamela L. Perrewe, Gerald R. Ferris, Dwight D. Frink, and William P. Anthony (2000), "Political Skill: An Antidote for Workplace Stressors," *Academy of Management Perspectives, 14* (3), 115–123.

28. Cameron Anderson, Daron L. Sharps, Christopher J. Soto, and Oliver P. John (2020), "People with Disagreeable Personalities (Selfish, Combative, and Manipulative) Do Not Have an Advantage in Pursuing Power at Work," *Proceedings of the National Academy of Science, 117* (37), 22780–22786. https://www.pnas.org/cgi/doi/10.1073/pnas.2005088117.

29. Jodi L. Short (1999), "Killing the Messenger: The Use of Nondisclosure Agreements to Silence Whistleblowers," *University of Pittsburgh Law Review, 60,* 1207–1234.

30. Dennis E. Clayson (2009), "Student Evaluations of Teaching: Are They Related to What Students Learn?" *Journal of Marketing Education, 31* (1), 16–30.

31. Bart De Langhe, Philip M. Fernbach, and Donald R. Lichtenstein (2016), "Navigating by the Stars: Investigating the Actual and Perceived Validity of Online User Ratings, *Journal of Consumer Research, 42,* 817–833.

32. Nalini Ambady, Frank J. Bernieri, and Jennifer A. Richeson (2000), "Toward a Histology of Social Behavior: Judgmental Accuracy from Thin Slices of the Behavioral Stream," *Advances in Experimental Social Psychology, 32,* 201–271; quote is from p. 201.

33. Alison Carmen (2015), "If You Judge People, You Have No Time to Love Them." https://www.psychologytoday.com/us/blog/the-gift -maybe/201504/if-you-judge-people-you-have-no-time-love-them.

34. Carmen, "If You Judge People."

35. BrainyQuote, https://brainyquote.com/quotes/walt_whitman_146892.

36. Barbara O'Brien, "The Buddhist Art of Nonjudgmental Judging Is Subtle," *The Guardian,* July 20, 2011.

37. Dana R. Carney (2020), "The Nonverbal Expression of Power, Status, and Dominance," *Current Opinion in Psychology, 33,* 256–264.

38. Jeffrey Pfeffer (2013), "You're Still the Same: Why Theories of Power Hold over Time and Across Contexts," *Academy of Management Perspectives, 27* (4), 269–280.

39. Sarah Lyons-Padilla et al., "Race Influences Professional Investors' Financial Judgments."

RULE 1

1. Samyukta Mullangi and Reshma Jagsi (2019), "Imposter Syndrome: Treat the Cause, Not the Symptom," *Journal of the American Medical Association, 322* (5), 403–404; quote is from p. 403.

2. George P. Chrousos, Alexios-Fotios A. Mentis, and Efthimios Dardiotis (2020), "Focusing on the Neuro-Psycho-Biological and Evolutionary Underpinnings of the Imposter Syndrome," *Frontiers in Psychology, 11,* 1553–1556.
3. Jeffrey Pfeffer, Christina T. Fong, Robert B. Cialdini, and Rebecca R. Portnoy (2006), "Overcoming the Self-Promotion Dilemma: Interpersonal Attraction and Extra Help as a Consequence of Who Sings One's Praises," *Personality and Social Psychology Bulletin, 32* (10), 1362–1374; quote is from p. 1362.
4. Dayrl J. Bem (1972), "Self-Perception Theory," *Advances in Experimental Social Psychology, 6,* 1–62; quote is from p. 1.
5. Gerald R. Salancik and Mary Conway (1975), "Attitude Inferences from Salient and Relevant Cognitive Content About Behavior," *Journal of Personality and Social Psychology, 32* (5), 829–840.
6. Deidre Boden, *The Business of Talk: Organizations in Action,* Cambridge: Polity Press, 1994.
7. Interview with Christina Troitino, July 9, 2020.
8. Rosabeth Moss Kanter (1979), "Power Failure in Management Circuits," *Harvard Business Review, 57* (4), 65–75; quote is from p. 65.
9. Deborah Gruenfeld, *Acting with Power: Why We Are More Powerful Than We Believe,* New York: Currency, 2020.
10. Malgorzata S., "An Excellent Resource for All Those Who Want to Learn How to Use Power Well," Amazon UK review, July 27, 2020, retrieved June 27, 2021.
11. Sam Borden, "Where Dishonesty Is Best Policy, U.S. Soccer Falls Short," *New York Times,* June 15, 2014.
12. Ann Schmidt, "How Arthur Blank, Bernie Marcus Co-founded Home Depot After Being Fired," Fox Business, August 2, 2020. https://www.foxbusiness.com/money/arthur-blank-bernie-marcus-home-depot-winning-formula.
13. Ann Schmidt, "How Netflix's Reed Hastings Overcame Failure While Leading His First Company," Fox Business, June 21, 2020. https://www.foxbusiness.com/money/netflix-ceo-reed-hastings-winning-formula.
14. Jeffrey Pfeffer and Gerald R. Salancik, *The External Control of Organizations: A Resource Dependence Persepctive,* Stanford, CA: Stanford Business Books, 2003.
15. Safi Bahcall, *Loonshots: How to Nurture the Crazy Ideas That Win Wars, Cure Diseases, and Transform Industries,* New York: St. Martin's Press, 2019; quotes are from pp. 57–59, emphasis added.

16. Jeffrey Pfeffer, *Power*, chapter two.
17. Peter Belmi and Kristin Laurin (2016), "Who Wants to Get to the Top? Class and Lay Theories About Power," *Journal of Personality and Social Psychology, 111* (4), 505–529.
18. Cameron Anderson and Gavin J. Kilduff (2009), "Why Do Dominant Personalities Attain Influence in Face-to-Face Groups? The Competence-Signaling Effects of Trait Dominance," *Journal of Personality and Social Psychology, 96* (2), 491–503.
19. Peter Belmi, Margaret A. Neal, David Reiff, and Rosemay Ulfe (2020), "The Social Advantages of Miscalibrated Individuals: The Relationship Between Social Class and Overconfidence and Its Implications for Class-Based Inequality," *Journal of Personality and Social Psychology, 118* (2), 254–282.
20. Musa Okwonga, *One of Them: An Eton College Memoir*, London: Unbound, 2021.
21. David Shariatmadari, "Musa Okwonga: 'Boys Don't Learn Shamelessness at Eton, It Is Where They Perfect It,'" *The Guardian*, April 10, 2021. https://www.theguardian.com/books/2021/apr/10/musa -okwonga-boys-dont-learn-shamelessness-at-eton-it-is-where-they -perfect-it.
22. Ascend Foundation, "Glass Ceiling for Asian Americans is 3.7 Times Harder to Crack," PR Newswire, May 6, 2015. https://prnewswire.com /news-release/glass-ceiling-foe-asian-americans-is37x-times-harder -to-crack-300078066.htm.
23. Sylvia Ann Hewlett, Ripa Rashid, Claire Ho, and Diana Forster, *Asians in America: Unleashing the Potential of the Model Minority*, New York: Center for Talent Innovation, 2011.
24. F. Pratto, L. M. Stallworth, and J. Sidanius (1997), "The Gender Gap: Differences in Political Attitudes and Social Dominance Orientation," *British Journal of Social Psychology, 36*, 49–68.
25. Lynn R. Offerman and Pamela E. Schrier (1985), "Social Influence Strategies: The Impact of Sex, Role and Attitudes Toward Power," *Personality and Social Psychology Bulletin, 11* (3).
26. Mats Alvesson and Katja Einola (2019), "Warning for Excessive Positivity: Authentic Leadership and Other Traps in Leadership Studies," *Leadership Quarterly, 30*, 383–395.
27. Adam Grant, "Unless You're Oprah, 'Be Yourself' Is Terrible Advice," *New York Times*, June 4, 2016. https://nyti.ms/22Fi3e0.
28. Kerry Roberts Gibson, Dana Harari, and Jennifer Carson Marr (2018), "When Sharing Hurts: How and Why Self-Disclosing Weakness

Undermines the Task-Oriented Relationships of Higher Status Disclosers," *Organizational Behavior and Human Decision Processes*, 144, 25–43; quote is from p. 25.

29. Gibson et al, "When Sharing Hurts," p. 25.
30. Gibson et al, "When Sharing Hurts," p. 38.
31. Herminia Ibarra, "The Authenticity Paradox," *Harvard Business Review*, January–February 2015. https://hbr.org/2015/01/the-authenticity-paradox.
32. Ibarra, "The Authenticity Paradox."
33. Ibarra, "The Authenticity Paradox."
34. Edward P. Lemay and Margaret S. Clark (2015), "Motivated Cognition in Relationships," *Current Opinion in Psychology, 1*, 72–75; quote is from p. 72.
35. Lemay and Clark, "Motivated Cognition in Relationships."
36. Charles F. Bond Jr. and Bella M. DePaulo (2008), "Individual Differences in Judging Deception: Accuracy and Bias," *Psychological Bulletin, 134* (4), 477–492; quote is from p. 477.
37. Charles F. Bond, Jr., & Bella M. DePaulo (2006). "Accuracy of Deception Judgments," Personality and Social Psychology Review, 10 (3), 214-224; quote is from p. 214.
38. Robert A. Caro, *The Path to Power*, New York: Knopf, 1982; Robert A. Caro, *Means of Ascent*, New York: Knopf, 1990; Robert A. Caro, *Master of the Senate*, New York: Knopf, 2002; Robert A. Caro, *The Passage of Power*, New York: Knopf, 2012.
39. James Richardson, *Willie Brown: A Biography*, Berkeley: University of California Press, 1996.
40. Robert B. Cialdini, *Influence: Science and Practice,* 5th ed., Boston: Allyn and Bacon, 2008.
41. Benjamin Schwarz, "Seeing Margaret Thatcher Whole," *New York Times,* November 12, 2019. https://www.nytimes.com/2019/11/12/books/review/margaret-thatcher-the-authorized-biography-herself-alone-charles-moore.html.
42. Any Cuddy (2009), "Just Because I'm Nice, Don't Assume I'm Dumb," *Harvard Business Review, 87* (2).
43. Teresa M. Amabile (1983), "Brilliant but Cruel: Perceptions of Negative Evaluators," *Journal of Experimental Social Psychology, 19* (2), 146–156.
44. Timothy A. Judge, Beth A. Livingston, and Charlice Hurst (2012), "Do Nice Guys—and Gals—Really Finish Last? The Joint Effects of Sex and Agreeableness on Income," *Journal of Personality and Social Psychology, 102* (2), 390–407.

45. Judge et al., "Do Nice Guys—and Gals—Really Finish Last?"
46. Anderson et al., "People with Disagreeable Personalities."

RULE 2

1. "Breaking Rules Makes You Seem Powerful," *Science Daily,* May 20, 2011. https://www.sciencedaily.com/releases/2011/05/110520092735.htm.
2. David Kipnis (1972), "Does Power Corrupt?" *Journal of Personality and Social Psychology, 24,* 33–41.
3. Gerben A. van Kleef, Astrid C. Homan, Catrin Finkenauer, Seval Gundemir, and Eftychia Stamkou (2011), "Breaking the Rules to Rise to Power: How Norm Violators Gain Power in the Eyes of Others," *Social Psychological and Personality Science, 2* (5), 500–507.
4. van Kleef et al., "Breaking the Rules," p. 500.
5. Jeffrey Pfeffer, "Jason Calacanis: A Case Study in Creating Resources," Stanford, CA: Graduate School of Business Case #OB104, November 11, 2019; quote is from p 3.
6. Pfeffer, "Jason Calacanis."
7. Kristen Meinzer and T. J. Raphael, "Here's What Happens After 'Surprise!'" *The Takeaway,* April 2, 2015. https://www.pri.org/stories/2015-04-02/heres-what-happens-after-surprise.
8. CPP Global, *Human Capital Report: Workplace Conflict and How Businesses Can Harness It to Thrive,* July 2008. http://img.en25.com/Web/CPP/Conflict_report.pdf.
9. Robert A. Caro, *The Power Broker: Robert Moses and the Fall of New York,* New York: Knopf, 1974; quote is from p. 217.
10. Caro, *The Power Broker,* p. 218.
11. Ivan Arreguin-Toft, *How the Weak Win Wars: A Theory of Asymmetric Conflict,* Cambridge, UK: Cambridge University Press, 2005.
12. Malcom Gladwell, "How David Beats Goliath," *New Yorker, 85* (13), May 11, 2009.
13. Susan Pulliam, Rebecca Elliott, and Ben Foldy, "Elon Musk's War on Regulators," *Wall Street Journal,* April 28, 2021.
14. Francis J. Flynn and Vanessa K. B. Lake (2008), "If You Need Help, Just Ask: Underestimating Compliance with Direct Requests for Help," *Journal of Personality and Social Psychology, 95* (1), 128–143; quote is from p. 140.
15. Jeffrey Pfeffer and Victoria Chang, "Keith Ferrazzi," Case #OB44, Stanford, CA: Graduate School of Business, November 15, 2003.

16. Reginald F. Lewis and Blair S. Walker, *Why Should White Guys Have All the Fun? How Reginald Lewis Created a Billion-Dollar Business Empire*, New York: Wiley, 1994.
17. Wikipedia, "Reginald Lewis," last modified September 10, 2021. http://en.wikipedia.org/wiki/Reginald_Lewis.

RULE 3

1. Nalini Ambady and Robert Rosenthal (1993), "Half a Minute: Predicting Teacher Evaluations from Thin Slices of Nonverbal Behavior and Physical Attractiveness," *Journal of Personality and Social Psychology, 64* (3), 431–441.
2. Raymond S. Nickerson (1998), "Confirmation Bias: A Ubiquitous Phenomenon in Many Guises," *Review of General Psychology, 2* (2), 175–220.
3. "How Fast Does the Average Person Speak?" Word Counter, June 2, 2016. https://wordcounter.net/blog/2016/06/02/101702_how-fast-average-person-speaks.html.
4. Steven A. Beebe (1974), "Eye Contact: A Nonverbal Determinant of Speaker Credibility," *Speech Teacher, 23* (1), 21–25.
5. Charles I. Brooks, Michael A. Church, and Lance Fraser (1986), "Effects of Duration of Eye Contact on Judgments of Personality Characteristics," *Journal of Social Psychology, 126* (1), 71–78.
6. Joylin M. Droney and Charles I. Brooks (1993), "Attributions of Self-Esteem as a Function of Duration of Eye Contact," *Journal of Social Psychology, 133* (5), 715–722.
7. Amy Cuddy, "Your Body Language May Shape Who You Are," TED, June 2012. https://www.ted.com/talks/amy_cuddy_your_body_language_may_shape_who_you_are?language=en.
8. Amy Cuddy, *Presence: Bringing Your Boldest Self to Your Biggest Challenges*, New York: Little, Brown Spark, 2005.
9. Ambady and Rosenthal, "Half a Minute."
10. Nicholas O. Rule and Nalini Ambady (2008), "The Face of Success: Inferences from Chief Executive Officers' Appearance Predict Company Profits," *Psychological Science, 19* (2), 109–111; quote is from p. 109.
11. Rule and Ambady, "The Face of Success," p. 110.
12. Nicholas O. Rule and Nalini Ambady (2009), "She's Got the Look: Inferences from Female Chief Executive Officers' Faces Predict Their Success," *Sex Roles, 61,* 644–652.
13. Quoted in Christian Hopp, Daniel Wentzel, and Stefan Rose (2020), "Chief Executive Officers' Appearance Predicts Company

Performance, or Does It? A Replication and Extension Focusing on CEO Successions," *Leadership Quarterly* (in press).

14. Arianna Bagnis, Ernesto Caffo, Carlo Cipolli, Allesandra De Palma, Garielle Farina, and Katia Mattarozzi (2020), "Judging Health Care Priority in Emergency Situations: Patient Facial Appearance Matters," *Social Science and Medicine, 260* (in press).

15. Peter Lundberg, Paul Nuystedt, and Dan-Olof Rooth (2014), "Height and Earnings: The Role of Cognitive and Noncognitive Skills," *Journal of Human Resources, 49* (1), 1141–1166.

16. See, e.g., Daniel S. Hammermesh, *Beauty Pays: Why Attractive People Are More Successful*, Princeton, NJ: Princeton University Press, 2011.

17. C. Pfeifer (2012), "Physical Attractiveness, Employment and Earnings," *Applied Economics Letters, 19*, 505–510.

18. P. C. Morrow, J. C. McElroy, B. G. Stamper, and M. A. Wilson (1990), "The Effects of Physical Attractiveness and Other Demographic Characteristics on Promotion Decisions," *Journal of Management, 16*, 723–736.

19. Kelly A. Nault, Marko Pitesa, and Stefan Thau (2020), "The Attractiveness Advantage at Work: A Cross-Disciplinary Integrative Review," *Academy of Management Annals, 14* (2), 1103–1139.

20. Leslie A. Zebrowitz and Joann M. Montepare (2008), "Social Psychological Face Perception: Why Appearance Matters," *Social and Personality Psychology Compass, 2/3*, 1497–1517; quote is from p. 1497.

21. Zebrowitz and Montepare, "Social Psychological Face Perception," p. 1498.

22. Baba Shiv and Alexander Fedorikhin (1999), "Heart and Mind in Conflict: The Interplay of Affect and Cognition in Consumer Decision Making," *Journal of Consumer Research, 26* (3), 278–292.

23. Dana R. Carney (2021), "Ten Things Every Manager Should Know About Nonverbal Behavior," *California Management Review, 63* (2), 5–22; quote is from p. 13.

24. Rob Goffee and Gareth Jones, *Why Should Anyone Be Led by You?* Boston: Harvard Review Press, 2006.

25. Larissa Z. Tiedens (2001), "Anger and Advancement Versus Sadness and Subjugation: The Effect of Negative Emotion Expressions on Social Status Conferral," *Journal of Personality and Social Psychology, 80* (1), 86–94; quotes are from p. 87.

26. Marwan Sinaceur and Larissa Z. Tidens (2006), "Get Mad and Get More Than Even: When and Why Anger Expression Is Effective in Negotiations," *Journal of Experimental Social Psychology, 42* (3), 314–322.

27. Karina Schumann (2018), "The Psychology of Offering an Apology: Understanding the Barriers to Apologizing and How to Overcome Them," *Current Directions in Psychological Science, 27* (2), 7–78; quote is from p. 76.

28. Tyler G. Okimoto, Michael Wenzel, and Kyli Hedrick (2013), "Refusing to Apologize Can Have Psychological Benefits (and We Issue No Mea Culpa for This Research Finding)," *European Journal of Social Psychology, 43*, 22–31, p. 29.

29. Shereen J. Cahudry and George Loewenstein (2019), "Thanking, Apologizing, Bragging, and Blaming: Responsibility Exchange Theory and the Currency of Communication," *Psychological Review, 126* (3), 313–344; quote is from p. 316.

30. Jennifer Latson, "How Poisoned Tylenol Became a Crisis-Management Teaching Model," *Time*, September 29, 2014, https://time.com/3423136 /tylenol-deaths-1982/.

31. Elaine Hatfield, John T. Cacioppo, and Richard L. Rapson, *Emotional Contagion*, Cambridge, UK: Cambridge University Press, 1994.

32. Timothy F. Jones, Allen S. Craig, Debbie Hoy, Elaine W. Gunter, David L. Ashley, Dana B. Barr, John W. Brock, and William Schaffner (2000), "Mass Psychogenic Illness Attributed to Toxic Exposure at a High School," *New England Journal of Medicine, 342* (2), 96–100.

33. Shirley Wang (2006), "Contagious Behavior," *Observer*, February 1. https://www.psychologicalscience.org/observer/contagious-behavior /comment-page-1.

34. Sigal G. Barsade, Constantinos G. V. Coutifaris, and Julianna Pillemer (2018), "Emotional Contagion in Organizational Life," *Research in Organizational Behavior, 18*, 137–151; quote is from p. 137.

35. Cameron Anderson, Sebastien Brion, Don A. Moore, and Jessica A. Kennedy (2012), "A Status-Enhancement Account of Overconfidence," *Journal of Personality and Social Psychology, 103* (4), 718–735.

36. Amy J. C. Cuddy, Caroline A. Wilmuth, Andy J. Yap, and Dana R. Carney (2015), "Preparatory Power Posing Affects Nonverbal Presence and Job Interview Performance," *Journal of Applied Psychology, 100* (4), 1286–1295.

37. Kerry Roberts Gibson, Dana Harari, and Jennifer Carson Marr (2018), "When Sharing Hurts: How and Why Self-Disclosing Weakness Undermines the Task-Oriented Relationships of Higher Status Disclosers," *Organizational Behavior and Human Decision Processes, 144*, 25–43; quote is from p. 25.

38. Gibson, Harari, and Marr, "When Sharing Hurts," p. 38.

39. Dana R. Carney (2020), "The Nonverbal Expression of Power, Status, and Dominance," *Current Opinion in Psychology, 33,* 256–264.

40. Judith Donath (2021), "Commentary: The Ethical Use of Powerful Words and Persuasive Machines," *Journal of Marketing, 85* (1), 160–162.

41. Wikipedia, "Flesch–Kincaid Readability Tests," last modified August 22, 2021. https://en.wikipedia.org/wiki/Flesch%E2%80%93Kincaid _readability_tests.

42. Lawrence A. Hosman (1989), "The Evaluative Consequences of Hedges, Hesitations, and Intensifiers: Powerful and Powerless Speech Styles," *Human Communication Research, 15* (3), 383–406.

43. Christian Unkelbach and Sarah C. Rom (2017), "A Referential Theory of the Repetition-Induced Truth Effect," *Cognition, 160,* 110–126; quote is from p. 110.

44. Jeffrey L. Foster, Thomas Huthwaite, Julia A. Yesberg, Maryanne Garry, and Elizabeth F. Loftus (2012), "Repetition, Not Number of Sources, Increases Both Susceptibility to Misinformation and Confidence in the Accuracy of Eyewitnesses" *Acta Psychologica, 139* (2), 320–326; quote is from p. 320.

45. "Donald Trump Says Muslims Support His Plan," *Jimmy Kimmel Live,* December 17, 2015. https://www.youtube.com/watch?v=Sqhg2FN zKHM.

46. Lindsey M. Grob, Renee A. Meyers, and Renee Schuh (1997), "Powerful/Powerless Language Use in Group Interactions: Sex Differences or Similarities? *Communication Quarterly, 45* (3), 282–303; quote is from p. 294.

47. Wikipedia, "Frank Abagnale," September 16, 2021. https://en .wikipedia.org/wiki/Frank_Abagnale.

48. Wikipedia, "Christian Gerhartsreiter," July 15, 2021. https://en .wikipedia.org/wiki/Christian_Gerhartsreiter.

RULE 4

1. Martin Kilduff and David Krackhardt (1994), "Bringing the Individual Back In: A Structural Analysis of the Internal Market for Reputation in Organizations," *Academy of Management Journal, 37* (1), 87–108.

2. Robert B. Cialdini, *Influence*; quote is from p. 45.

3. Robert B. Cialdini, Richard J. Borden, Avril Thorne, Marcus Randall Walker, Stephen Freeman, and Lloyd Reynolds Sloan (1976), "Basking in Reflected Glory: Three (Football) Field Studies," *Journal of Personality and Social Psychology, 34* (3), 366–375.

4. Jeffrey Pfeffer, "Tristan Walker: The Extroverted Introvert," Case #OB93, Stanford, CA: Graduate School of Business, Stanford University, October 26, 2016; quote is from pp. 1–2.

5. Victoria Chang, Kimberly Elsbach, and Jeffrey Pfeffer, "Jeffrey Sonnenfeld: The Fall from Grace," Case #OB34A, Stanford, CA: Graduate School of Business, Stanford University, August 21, 2006.

6. Josh Barro, "Black Mark for Fiorina Campaign in Criticizing Yale Dean," *New York Times,* September 23, 2015.

7. Philip Weiss, "Is Emory Prof Jeffrey Sonnenfeld Caught in a New Dreyfus Affair?" *New York Observer,* May 17, 1999.

8. Michael Mattis, "Style Counsel: Willie Brown on Dressing the Man," https://www.cbsnews.com/news/style-counsel-willie-brown-on -dressing-the-man/.

9. Jason Calacanis, *Angel: How to Invest in Technology Startups,* New York: Harper Business, 2017.

10. Lee A. Iacocca and William Novak, *Iacocca: An Autobiography,* New York: Bantam Dell, 1984.

11. Jack Welch with John A. Byrne, *Jack: Straight from the Gut,* New York: Business Plus, 2001.

12. Pfeffer et al., "Overcoming the Self-Promotion Dilemma."

13. Pfeffer, "Tristan Walker," p. 11.

14. Megan Elisabeth Anderson and Jeffrey Pfeffer, "Nuria Chinchilla: The Power to Change Workplaces," Case #OB67, Stanford, CA: Graduate School of Business, Stanford University, February 14, 2011; quote is from p. 13.

15. Anderson and Pfeffer, "Nuria Chinchilla."

16. Pfeffer, "Jason Calacanis"; quote is from pp. 4–5.

17. Pfeffer, "Jason Calacanis"; pp. 12–13.

18. Jeffrey Pfeffer, "Sadiq Gillani's Airline Career Takes Off: Strategy in Action," Case #OB95, Stanford, CA: Graduate School of Business, Stanford University, November 30, 2018.

19. Ibid., quote is from p. 13.

20. Richard W. Halstead (2000), "From Tragedy to Triumph: Counselor as Companion on the Hero's Journey," *Counseling and Values, 44* (2), 100–106; quote is from p. 100.

21. Jim Collins, *Good to Great: Why Some Companies Make the Leap and Others Don't,* New York: Harper Business, 2001.

22. Annabelle R. Roberts, Emma E. Levine, and Ovul Sezer (2020), "Hiding Success," *Journal of Personality and Social Psychology, 120* (5), 1261–1286.

RULE 5

1. Wikipedia, "Omid Kordestani," last modified September 7, 2021. https://en.wikipedia.org/wiki/Omid_Kordestani.
2. Alistair Barr, "Google Pays Returning Chief Business Officer $130 Million," *Wall Street Journal*, April 23, 2015. https://www.wsj.com/articles/google-pays-returning-chief-business-officer-130-million-1429828322.
3. Jeffrey Pfeffer and Ross Walker, *People Are the Name of the Game: How to Be More Successful in Your Career—and Life*, Pennsauken Township, NJ: BookBaby, 2013.
4. Keith Ferrazzi with Tahl Raz, *Never Eat Alone: And Other Secrets to Success, One Relationship at a Time* (2nd expanded ed.), New York: Currency, 2014.
5. Jiuen Pai, Sanford E. DeVoe, and Jeffrey Pfeffer (2020), "How Income and the Economic Evaluation of Time Affect Who We Socialize with Outside of Work," *Organizational Behavior and Human Decision Processes, 161*, 158–175.
6. Ivan Misner, "How Much Time Should You Spend Networking?" August 9, 2018. https://ivanmisner.com/time-spend-networking.
7. Daniel Kahneman, Alan B. Krueger, David A. Schkade, Norbert Schwarz, and Arthur A. Stone (2004), "A Survey Method for Characterizing Daily Life Experience: The Day Reconstruction Method," *Science, 5702*, 1776–1780.
8. Tiziana Casciaro, Francesco Gino, and Maryam Kouchaki (2014), "The Contaminating Effects of Building Instrumental Ties: How Networking Can Make Us Feel Dirty," *Administrative Science Quarterly, 59* (4), 705–735.
9. Pai et al., "How Income and the Economic Evaluation," p. 158. The study referred to is C. R. Wanberg, R. Kanfer, and J. T. Banas (2000), "Predictors and Outcomes of Networking Intensity Among Unemployed Job Seekers," *Journal of Applied Psycholoy, 85*, 491–503.
10. Jeffrey Pfeffer, "Ross Walker's Path to Power," Case #OB79, Stanford, CA: Stanford Graduate School of Business, February 7, 2011; quote is from p. 14.
11. Hans-Georg Wolff and Klaus Moser (2009), "Effects of Networking on Career Success: A Longitudinal Study," *Journal of Applied Psychology, 94* (1), 196–206.
12. Torstein Nesheim, Karen Modesta Olsen, and Alexander Modsen Sandvik (2017), "Never Walk Alone: Achieving Working Performance

Through Networking Ability and Autonomy," *Employee Relations, 39* (2), 240–253.

13. Samuel Y. Todd, Kenneth J. Harris, Ranida B. Harris, and Anthony R. Wheeler (2010), "Career Success Implications of Political Skill," *Journal of Social Psychology, 149* (3), 279–304.

14. Munyon et al., "Political Skill and Work Outcomes."

15. Carter Gibson, Jay H. Hardy III, and M. Ronald Buckley (2014), "Understanding the Role of Networking in Organizations, *Career Development International 19* (2), 146–161.

16. Jennifer Miller, "Want to Meet Influential New Yorkers? Invite Them to Dinner," *New York Times,* October 9, 2013. https://www.nytimes.com/2013/10/10/fashion/want-to-meet-influential-new-yorkers-invite-them-to-dinner.html.

17. Michael I. Norton, Daniel Mochon, and Dan Ariely (2012), "The IKEA Effect: When Labor Leads to Love," *Journal of Consumer Psychology, 22* (3), 453–460.

18. Mark S. Granovetter, *Getting a Job: A Study of Contacts and Careers,* Chicago: University of Chicago Press, 1974.

19. Mark S. Granovetter (1973), "The Strength of Weak Ties," *American Journal of Sociology, 78,* 1360–1380.

20. J. E. Perry-Smith (2006), "Social Yet Creative: The Role of Social Relationships in Facilitating Individual Creativity," *Academy of Management Journal, 49,* 85–101.

21. Gillian M. Sandstrom and Elizabeth W. Dunn (2014), "Social Interactions and Well-Being: The Surprising Power of Weak Ties," *Personality and Social Psychology Bulletin, 40* (7), 910–922; quote is from p. 918.

22. Ronald S. Burt (2004), "Structural Holes and Good Ideas," *American Journal of Sociology, 110* (2), 349–399; quote is from p. 349.

23. Burt, "Structural Holes and Good Ideas."

24. Ronald S. Burt (2000), "The Network Structure of Social Capital," *Research in Organizational Behavior, 22,* 345–423.

25. Ronald S. Burt (2007), "Secondhand Brokerage: Evidence on the Importance of Local Structure for Managers, Bankers, and Analysts," *Academy of Management Journal, 50* (1), 119–148; quote is from p. 119.

26. Jeffrey Pfeffer, "Zia Yusuf at SAP: Having Impact," Case #OB73, February 3, 2009, Stanford, CA: Graduate School of Business, Stanford University.

27. Herminia Ibarra (1993), "Network Centrality, Power, and Innovation Involvement: Determinants of Technical and Administrative Roles," *Academy of Management Journal, 36* (3), 471–501.

28. Myung-Ho Chung, Jeehye Park, Hyoung Koo Moon, and Hongseok Oh (2011), "The Multilevel Effects of Network Embeddedness on Interpersonal Citizenship Behavior," *Small Group Research*, 42 (6), 730–760.
29. Brian Mullen, Craig Johnson, and Eduardo Salas (1991), "Effects of Communication Network Structure: Components of Positional Centrality," *Social Networks*, 13 (2), 169–185.
30. Alvin W. Gouldner (1960), "The Norm of Reciprocity: A Preliminary Statement," *American Sociological Review*, 25, 161–178.
31. Ronald S. Burt and Don Ronchi (2007), "Teaching Executives to See Social Capital: Results from a Field Experiment," *Social Science Research*, 36 (3), 1156–1183; quote is from p. 1156.

RULE 6

1. The National Security Archive, "Episode 13: Make Love, Not War (The Sixties)," George Washington University, January 10, 1999. https://nsarchive2.gwu.edu/coldwar/interviews/episode-13/valenti1.html.
2. Per-Ola Karlsson, Martha Turner, and Peter Gassmann (2019), "Succeeding the Long-Serving Legend in the Corner Office, *Strategy + Business*," Summer 2019, Issue 95. https://www.strategy-business.com/article/Succeeding-the-long-serving-legend-in-the-corner-office.
3. Matt Barnum, "How Long Does a Big-City Superintendent Last? Longer Than You Might Think," *Chalkbeat*, May 8, 2018. https://www.chalkbeat.org/2018/5/8/21105877/how-long-does-a-big-city-superintendent-last-longer-than-you-might-think.
4. https://www.healthcarefinancenews.com/news/hospital-ceo-turnover-rate-dipped-2019-first-tiime-five-years.
5. The material in this section is primarily drawn from Jeffrey Pfeffer, "Amir Rubin: Success from the Beginning," Case #OB90, January 6, 2015, Stanford, CA: Graduate School of Business, Stanford University.
6. Stanford Health Care, "Stanford Health Care-Stanford Hospital Named to U.S. News & World Report's 2015-16 Best Hospitals Honor Roll," July 21, 2015. https://stanfordhealthcare.org/newsroom/news/press-releases/2015/us-news-2015-16.html.
7. Sara Mosie, "The Stealth Chancellor," *New York Times*, August 31, 1997. https://www.nytimes.com/1997/08/31/magazine/the-stealth-chancellor.html.
8. Jeffrey Pfeffer, "Kent Thiry and DaVita: Leadership Challenges in Building and Growing a Great Company," Case #OB54, May 22, 2006,

Stanford, CA: Graduate School of Business, Stanford University; quote is from p. 5.

9. C. Edward Fee and Charles J. Hadlock (2004), "Management Turnover Across the Corporate Hierarchy," *Journal of Accounting and Economics,* 37 (1), 3–38.

10. Idalene F. Kesner and Dan R. Dalton (1994), "Top Management Turnover and CEO Succession: An Investigation of the Effects of Turnover on Performance," *Journal of Management Studies,* 31 (5), 701–713.

11. James Richardson, *Willie Brown: A Biography,* Berkeley: University of California Press, 1996; quote is from p. 278.

12. Richardson, *Willie Brown,* pp. 278–279.

13. Wikipedia, "Frances K. Conley," last modified July 21, 2021. https://en .wikipedia.org/wiki/Frances_K._Conley.

14. "Citing Sexism, Stanford Doctor Quits," *New York Times,* June 4, 1991, p. A22.

15. Goodreads, "Niccolò Machiavelli." https://www.goodreads.com /quotes/22338-it-is-much-safer-to-be-feared-than-loved-because.

16. Paul Goldberer, "Robert Moses, Master Builder, Is Dead at 92," *New York Times,* July 30, 1981, p. A1. https://www.nytimes.com/1981/07/30 /obituaries/robert-moses-master-builder-is-dead-at-92.html.

17. Caro, *The Power Broker,* p. 449.

18. Caro, *The Power Broker,* p. 986.

19. Sydney Sarachan, "The Legacy of Robert Moses," January 17, 2013. https://web.archive.org/web/20180617043637/http://www.pbs.org /wnet/need-to-know/environment/the-legacy-of-robert-moses/.

20. Sydney Sarachan, "The Legacy of Robert Moses," January 17, 2013. *Need to Know on PBS.*

21. Emily Stewart, "Mark Zuckerberg Is Essentially Untouchable at Facebook," Vox, December 29, 2018. https://www.vox.com/technology /2018/11/19/18099011/mark-zuckerberg-facebook-stock-nyt-wsj.

22. Mengqi Sun, "More U.S. Companies Separating Chief Executive and Chairman Roles," *Wall Street Journal,* January 23, 2019.

23. Connie Bruck, "The Personal Touch," *New Yorker,* August 6, 2001.

24. Paul Goldberger, "Robert Moses, Master Builder, Is Dead at 92," *New York Times,* July 30, 1981, p. A1.

RULE 7

1. Bahcall, *Loonshots*; quote is from p. 56.

2. Glenn Thrush, Jo Becker, and Danny Hakim, "Tap Dancing with Trump: Lindsey Graham's Quest for Relevance," *New York Times,* August 14, 2021. https://www.nytimes.com/2021/08/14/us/politics /lindsey-graham-donald-trump.html.

3. Mark Leibovich, "How Lindsey Graham Went from Trump Skeptic to Trump Sidekick," *New York Times,* February 25, 2019. https://www .nytimes.com/2019/02/25/magazine/lindsey-graham-what-happened -grukmp.html.

4. Leibovich, "How Lindsey Graham Went from Trump Skeptic to Trump Sidekick."

5. Thrush et al., "Tap Dancing with Trump."

6. David G. Winter (1988), "The Power Motive in Women—and Men," *Journal of Personality and Social Psychology, 54* (3), 510–519.

7. Wiktionary, "The nail that sticks out gets hammered down," last modified August 6, 2020. https://en.wiktionary.org/wiki/the_nail_that _sticks_out_gets_hammered_down.

8. Wikipedia, "Tall Poppy Syndrome," last modified September 9, 2021. https://en.wikipedia.org/wiki/Tall_poppy_syndrome.

9. https://biblehub.com/matthew/25-29.htm.

10. Robert K. Merton (1988), "The Matthew Effect in Science, II: Cumulative Advantage and the Symbolism of Intellectual Property," *Isis, 79,* 606–623; quote is from p. 606.

11. Michelle L. Dion, Jane Lawrence Sumner, and Sara McLaughlin Mitchell (2018), "Gendered Citation Patterns Across Political Science and Social Science Methodology Fields," *Political Analysis, 26,* 312–327.

12. Matjaz Perc (2014), "The Matthew Effect in Empirical Data," *Journal of the Royal Society Interface, 11,* http://dx.doi.org/10.1098/rsif.2014.0378.

13. See, for instance, Niklas Karlsson, George Loewenstein, and Duane Seppi (2009), "The Ostrich Effect: Selective Attention to Information, *Journal of Risk and Uncertainty, 38,* 95–115; Jack Fyock and Charles Stangor (1994), "The Role of Memory Biases in Stereotype Maintenance," *British Journal of Social Psychology, 33* (3), 331–343.

14. Alison R. Fragale, Benson Rosen, Carol Xu, and Iryna Merideth (2009), "The Higher They Are, the Harder They Fall: The Effects of Wrongdoer Status on Observer Punishment Recommendations and Intentionality Attributions," *Organizational Behavior and Human Decision Processes, 108* (1), 53–65.

15. Scott D. Griffin, Jonathan Bundy, Joseph F. Porac, James B. Wade, and Dennis P. Quinn (2013), "Falls from Grace and the Hazards of High

Status: The 2009 British MP Expense Scandal and Its Impact on Parliamentary Elites," *Administrative Science Quarterly, 58* (3), 313–345.

16. Hannah Riley Bowles and Michele Gelfand (2010), "Status and the Evaluation of Workplace Deviance," *Psychological Science, 21* (1), 49–54.

17. Evan Polman, Nathan C. Pettit, and Batia M. Wiesenfeld (2013), "Effects of Wrongdoer Status on Moral Licensing," *Journal of Experimental Social Psychology, 49* (4), 614–623.

18. Jesse Eisinger, *The Chickenshit Club: Why the Justice Department Fails to Prosecute Executives*, New York: Simon & Schuster, 2017.

19. James Kwak, "America's Top Prosecutors Used to Go After Top Executives. What Changed?" *New York Times*, July 5, 2017.

20. Julie Creswell with Naomi Prins, "The Emperor of Greed: With the Help of His Bankers, Gary Winnick Treated Global Crossing as His Personal Cash Cow—Until the Company Went Bankrupt," CNN Money, June 24, 2002. https://money.cnn.com/magazines/fortune /fortune_archive/2002/06/24/325183/.

21. Chris Gaither, Jonathan Peterson, and David Colker, "Founder Escapes Charges in Global Crossing Failure," *Los Angeles Times*, December 14, 2004.

22. William D. Cohan, "Michael Milken Invented the Modern Junk Bond, Went to Prison, and Then Became One of the Most Respected People on Wall Street," *Insider,* May 2, 2017. https://www.businessinsider .com/michael-milken-life-story-2017-5.

23. Ibid.

24. Ann Friedman, "Martha Stewart's Best Lesson: Don't Give a Damn," *New York Magazine*, March 14, 2013.

25. Jodi Kantor, Mike McIntire, and Vanessa Friedman, "Jeffrey Epstein Was a Sex Offender. The Powerful Welcomed Him Anyway," *New York Times*, July 13, 2019.

26. David Enrich, "How Jeffrey Epstein Got Away with It," *New York Times,* July 13 2021. https://www.nytimes.com/2021/07/13/books /review/perversion-of-justice-julie-k-brown.html.

27. Duncan Riley, "Employee Management Software Startup Rippling Raises $145M on Unicorn Valuation," SiliconAngle, August 4, 2020. https://siliconangle.com/2020/08/04/employee-management-software -startup-rippling-raises-145m-on-unicorn-valuation/.

28. Nathaniel Popper, "Sex Scandal Toppled a Silicon Valley Chief. Investors Say, So What?" *New York Times*, July 27, 2018.

29. Leslie Berlin, "Mike Isaac's Uber Book Has Arrived," *New York Times*, September 6, 2019.
30. Dacher Keltner, Deborah H. Gruenfeld, and Cameron Anderson (2003), "Power, Approach, and Inhibition," *Psychological Review, 110* (2), 265–284.
31. Cameron Anderson and Adam D. Galinsky (2006), "Power, Optimism, and Risk Taking," *European Journal of Social Psychology, 36* (4), 511–536.
32. Brent L. Hughes and Jamil Zaki (2015), "The Neuroscience of Motivated Cognition," *Trends in Cognitive Sciences, 19* (2), 62–64; quote is from p. 62.
33. Hughes and Zaki, "The Neuroscience of Motivated Cognition."
34. Arie W. Kruganski, Katarzyna Jasko, Maxim Milyavsky, Marina Chernikova, David Webber, Antonio Pierro, and Daniela di Santo (2018), "Cognitive Consistency Theory in Social Psychology: A Paradigm Reconsidered," *Psychological Inquiry, 29* (2), 45–59.
35. Barry M. Staw, "Attribution of the 'Causes' of Performance: A General Alternative Interpretation of Cross-Sectional Research on Organizations," *Organizational Behavior and Human Performance, 13* (3), 414–432; quote is from p. 414.
36. Amit Bhattacharjee, Jonathan Z. Berman, and Americus Reed II (2013), "Tip of the Hat, Wag of the Finger: How Moral Decoupling Enables Consumers to Admire and Admonish," *Journal of Consumer Research, 39*, 1167–1184.
37. Bhattacharjee et al., "Tip of the Hat," p. 1168; the Bandura article to which this quote refers includes Albert Bandura, Claudio Barbaranelli, Gian V. Caprara, and Concetta Pastorelli (1996), "Mechanisms of Moral Disengagement in the Exercise of Moral Agency," *Journal of Personality and Social Psychology, 71* (2), 364–374.
38. Ibid.
39. Ibid.
40. Victoria Chang and Jeffrey Pfeffer, "Dr. Laura Esserman (A)," Case #OB42A, Stanford, CA: Graduate School of Business, Stanford University, September 30, 2003; quote is from p 4.
41. Jeffrey Sonnenfeld, *The Hero's Farewell: What Happens When CEOs Retire*, New York: Oxford University Press, 1988.
42. Nick Bilton, "All Is Fair in Love and Twitter," *New York Times*, October 9, 2013. The material on Dorsey and Twitter comes from this source.

43. Bilton, "All Is Fair."
44. Jelani Cobb, "Harvey Weinstein, Bill Cosby and the Cloak of Charity," *New Yorker*, October 14, 2017.
45. Renae Merle, "In Decades Before Pardon, Michael Milken Launched 'Davos' Competitor and Showered Millions on Charities," *Washington Post*, February 21, 2020.
46. WebMD, "2014 People's Choice: Martha Stewart," accessed September 16, 2021. https://www.webmd.com/healthheroes/2014-peoples-choice-martha-stewart.
47. Winnick Family Foundation, "About," accessed September 16, 2021. http://www.winnickfamilyfoundation.com/about.html.
48. Quote Investigator, "Winning Isn't Everything; It's the Only Thing," March 13, 2017. https://quoteinvestigator.com/2017/03/13/winning/.

CODA

1. Pfeffer and Sutton, *The Knowing-Doing Gap*.
2. Jeffrey Pfeffer, *Power*.
3. *Encyclopedia Britannica*, "Marcus Brutus." https://www.britannica.com/topic/Marcus-Brutus.
4. See, e.g., Robert I. Sutton and Andrew Hargadon (1996), "Brainstorming Groups in Context: Effectiveness in a Product Design Firm," *Administrative Science Quarterly*, 41 (4), 685–718.
5. Robert B. Zajonc (1965), "Social Facilitation," *Science, 149* (3681), 269–274.
6. Anthony J. Mento, Robert P. Steel, and Ronald J. Karren (1987), "A Meta-Analytic Study of the Effects of Goal Setting on Task Performance: 1966–1984," *Organizational Behavior and Human Decision Processes, 39* (1), 52–83.

INDEX

Schultz, Howard, 167
Schwarzman, Stephen, 167
Scott, Kim, 167
"The Scuffed Halls of Ivy" (TV
    episode), 92
Seabury Consulting, 101
SEC (U.S. Securities and Exchange
    Commission), 153
self-confidence, and appearing
    powerful, 78–80
self-disclosure, 80
self-image, 19–25
Shaw Communications, 140
Sheinberg, Sidney, 140
Sheth, Jagdish, 28
Shiv, Baba, 72
Silicon Alley 100, 100
Silicon Alley Reporter (publication), 100
Silverberg, Gerald, 136
Simon Wiesenthal Center (Jerusalem),
    170
60 Minutes, 57, 92, 93
Sloan, Alfred P., 166
Snapchat, 140
soccer, 26–27
Soccernomics (Kuper), 27
social class issues, 30–32
social dominance orientation, 33
Social Finance (personal finance
    company), 156
social media, 123
*Social Psychological and Personality
    Science* (journal), 48
social relationships, 111–113
Sonnenfeld, Jeffrey, 91–92, 164–165
South Carolina, 144
SpaceX, 55
Square, 93
"Squawk Alley" (news show), 100
standing out, 56–58, 99–101
Stanford business school, 16, 20, 24,
    28, 30, 45, 47, 102, 107, 136
Stanford Graduate School of Business,
    1, 179
Stanford Healthcare, 129, 133, 135
Stanford Medical School, 135, 136
Stanford Operating System, 129–131
Stanford University, 1, 3, 73, 84, 109,
    179. *see also* Stanford business
    school
Starbucks, 167
Staw, Barry, 160

Stephanopoulos, George, 155
Stern, Howard, 100
Stewart, Martha, 46, 154, 167, 170
Suárez, Luis, 26–27
success, 143–171
    and cumulative advantage,
        148–151
    and following the rules of power,
        145–148
    and insulation of wrongdoers,
        151–158
    and motivated cognition, 158–165
    and writing of history, 165–170
Sundance Film Festival, 45
surprise, neurobiology of, 52
Suster, Mark, 99
Syracuse University, 170

T
taking credit for your work, 103–105
Taking Stock (newsletter), 89
Tavern on the Green (New York City),
    138
Taylor Estate (East Islip, N.Y.), 54
teambuilding, 132–136
Team Positivity Contagion, 47
TED talks, 69, 102
telling your story, 90–93
tenure, of leaders, 128
Teresa, Mother, 13
Tesla, Inc., 55
Thatcher, Margaret, 40
Theranos, 93, 155
Thiel, Peter, 167
Thiry, Kent, 133
This Week in Startups (podcast), 94–95
Thrive Global, 173
Tiedens, Larissa, 75–76
Time magazine, 34
time management, and networking,
    123–125
TLC Beatrice International Holdings,
    60
Total Renal Care, 133
Triborough Bridge (New York City),
    137
Troitino, Christina, 24–25, 27, 45–48,
    50, 53
Trump, Donald, 50, 75, 83, 143–144,
    159
Twain, Mark, 92
Twitter, 55, 93, 107, 168–169

ABOUT THE AUTHOR

 **Jeffrey Pfeffer** (www.jeffreypfeffer.com) is the Thomas D. Dee II Professor of Organizational Behavior at the Stanford Graduate School of Business. Pfeffer is the author or coauthor of sixteen books on topics including power in organizations, managing people, evidence-based management, and *The Knowing-Doing Gap*.

Pfeffer received his PhD from Stanford and taught at the University of Illinois at Urbana-Champaign and the University of California, Berkeley, before returning to Stanford in 1979 as a full professor.

As the author of more than 150 articles and book chapters, Pfeffer has won numerous awards for his scholarly research, including an honorary doctorate from Tilburg University in the Netherlands.

Pfeffer has taught seminars in forty countries and has been a visiting professor at Harvard Business School, London Business School, Singapore Management University, and for many years, IESE in Barcelona. He has served on the board of directors of several human capital software companies as well as other public and private company and nonprofit boards. He lives in Hillsborough, California.